Obaedo

A Redemption

Story of a young woman and her overcoming through Christ her many travails.

This novel is a work of fiction. Names, characters, places and incidents are either the product of the author's imagination, or are used fictitiously. Apart from actual historical facts, any resemblance to actual events or locales or persons, living or dead, is entirely coincidental

www.kingdompublishers.co.uk

Obaedo- A Redemption.

Copyright © Chima Cliff Chima

All rights reserved.

No part of this book may be reproduced in any form by photocopying or any electronic or mechanical means, including information storage or retrieval systems, without permission in writing from both the copyright owner and the publisher of the book. The right of Chima Cliff Chima to be identified as the author of this work has been asserted by him in accordance with the Copyright, Designs and Patents Act 1988 and any subsequent amendments thereto. A catalogue record for this book is available from the British Library.

ISBN: 978-1-913247-00-3

1st Edition by Kingdom Publishers
Kingdom Publishers
London, UK.

For Sharon and Elijah.

They were there in my transition hours.

And to Leena

Contents

Chapter 1 - *Mint Notes.* — 5

Chapter 2 - *A Unique Presence.* — 14

Chapter 3 - *Snack on The table.* — 17

Chapter 4 - *Clean Ways.* — 21

Chapter 5 - *Charisma.* — 30

Chapter 6 - *Testing the Waters.* — 49

Chapter 7 - *Showing Care.* — 64

Chapter 8 - *Politeness.* — 76

Chapter 9 - *Politeness Still.* — 88

Chapter 10 - *Best Friend.* — 108

Chapter 11 - *Waters over my soul* — 118

Chapter 12 - *Saving for my Queen.* — 124

Chapter 13 - *Dark Waters.* — 142

Chapter 14 - *Heart of a slave.* — 156

Chapter 15 - *Breaking Point…Dawn.* — 180

Chapter 16 - *A Plane in the cloud.* — 195

Chapter 1
Mint Notes.

Finally, the graduation ceremony came. After six years of secondary school education at Edokpolor Grammar School, Benin City, in mid-Western Nigeria, Obaedo was graduating. It was August 30th, 1999 and after many years of military dictatorship, Nigeria had just returned to constitutional rule. The graduation, the first for a very long time under a civilian administration was made a continuation of the nation's celebration of the military leaving the affairs of governance. The school authorities organized series of events to celebrate it. There was a football match between the graduating students' team and a selected team picked from other students. The day before the graduation ceremony, the Head of Department of Political Science of the University of Benin, Professor John Otuokpaishan Akhigbe was invited to give a Talk on Nigeria's Political Prospects to the graduating students. Professor Akhigbe, a bold and frank speaker in several major public events, traced Nigeria's political history through the lens of a political scientist, holding his audience spellbound as he related national events with his booming voice.

"...Nigeria was a British creation. We have not been able to re-create this nation according to our own image. All serious attempts have been stifled. The British just brought distinct ethnic nationalities of almost racial incompatibility and merged them together for their own personal interest without the decency of consulting us the people via a referendum. The northern Muslims, generally placid and implicitly obedient were favoured by the British in preference to others: the enlightened Westerners, the Yoruba; the very industrious Easterners, the Igbos and the other ethnic minorities in the Eastern region. This tilt in political preference was laid into the nation's foundation at independence. Certainly after independence, the northern elite who got the military and political power, pushed through well planned successive acts to bring the entire nation under their dominance. Through political intrigues and crafty alliances, the neutralizing of the western region's homegrown political leadership was achieved. Then the military was deployed to quell northern minorities' agitation. This northern power elite under the guise of exercising governmental authority cleared the coast to become the new colonial masters of the young nation. They did not reckon that in the past, instances of such political oppression got things to inevitably boil over. And it did. An idealist young army Major from a minority tribe in the Mid-West region was planning for them. He led a warmly accepted revolution on January 15, 1966, struck deep to wipe out the tainted political class and spearhead a national rebirth. The entire nation rose as one man to applaud the demise of that disgraceful bunch of civilian rulers. I was in the North then and I witnessed the joyful celebrations. The revolutionary plans were however not fully executed by some of those given responsibilities, some just absconded and some things were bungled. The revolutionary attempt was then crushed by powerful centrifugal forces beyond the young Major. Reprisals from Northerners against Easterners would follow, from an instigated and later blatant misreading of the attempted Coup d'état. The BBC played a most shameful role to incite the wanton tribal killings.

During the months of May, July, August, and September, 1966, Northern Nigerian soldiers and civilians planned and sadistically, brutally and in cold blood, slaughtered thousands of the Igbos and other Southerners. Innocent people including children, helpless women, defenseless, were murdered in cold blood. There were acts of savagery as women in actual labour and their unborn children were killed. The mob plundered and looted, they raped women freely. It is a miracle that the Igbo ethnic group was not totally wiped out by the satanic forces unleashed in Nigeria in 1966. In his book, *My Command*, General Olusegun Obasanjo gave this verdict of history, 'The lack of planning and the vengeful intention of the second coup manifested itself in the chaos, confusion and the scale of unnecessary killings which spread throughout the country. Even the authors of the coup could not stem the general lawlessness and disorder, the senseless looting and killing that spread through the north like wildfire.'

The then Head of State, Lt.Col. Yakubu Gowon was also helpless to stop the wild killings as he told the nation in a broadcast in September 1966, 'I receive complaints daily that up till now Easterners living in the North are being killed and molested and their property looted. It appears that it is going beyond reason and is now at a point of recklessness and irresponsibility'

In the succeeding months, the Hausa/Fulani controlled Government of Nigeria, while most of the world looked away but with the complete support of the British in the form of military and political aid, took war to the Eastern region to totally subjugate the Igbos. It was shocking for a Christian country like Britain to help a Moslem group militarily to crush Christians in the east of Nigeria. But it happened. It all boils down to selfish and wicked interests. Principles be damned. Nigeria's political elite since independence from Britain in 1960 have always tended towards corrupt and parasitic practices with a heartless disregard for the state of the poor masses. The hopeless mismanagement of the economy has led to continual unemployment even as cost of living continues to rise. It is surprising when one realises that those who have wrecked destruction on this country and pauperized its people are indeed nationals of this country. It is unexplainable. It may be explained by Chinua Achebe's posit that it has to do with a certain incomprehensible trait in the Negro. Nigeria's first attempt at democratic rule immediately after independence and later in 1979-1983 showed the real character of the political class. The treasury became a bazaar for politicians with all kind of proposals and projects with little relevance to the people. The Nigerian military which intervened in politics on the pretext of correcting the crass misdeeds of the political class further despoiled the country and compounded its complexity. Disillusionment filled the land and political antagonism among different groups worsened. This last transition to democratic rule was long and tortuous with the northern military umpires clearly having interest in transmuting themselves into a new civilian leadership over the country. Having fought a vicious civil war against the Igbo and won, this northern-led military elite took over the destiny of this nation and have up to this day acted as patrons in the dispensing of power and of the nation's enormous wealth. Largely uneducated, these military rulers and their civilian collaborators have imposed their will upon this nation and unleashed harsh and intolerable conditions on its people. Many of those now parading as the new democratic leaders have been military collaborators and the Independent National Electoral Commission, INEC, looked away at the obvious criminal records of many contestants. Many of these later won elective offices through less than honest means. It is therefore too early to say if this present bunch of civilian leaders will bring real changes and progress to Nigerians as their antecedents are scary…"

He took questions from the graduating students and posed for a group photograph afterwards. The students went home to prepare for their big day.

Obaedo had done very well in her studies throughout her secondary school education and her West African Examination Council [WAEC] School certificate result truly demonstrated her academic excellence. Her father, Chief Edward Ojiefo Ahamioje was overjoyed. He came with his three wives and some of their children to celebrate with Obaedo. They all turned out in colourful dresses and were all in a radiant mood. The sky was blue above and along with the different colourful wears of the attendees, the whole place was one big sea of vivacity. Vendors of fast food, ice cream, cold drinks, snacks and other local edibles mixed freely with the crowd in the compound. Commercial photographers were making brisk business as well as traditional Yoruba praise singers beating their drums expertly. Many a feet of parents took to dancing when the praise singers came to them drumming and singing. It had rained heavily during the dark night and flood had taken over the city. However by morning, the earth had opened her mouth and drank up the water. Now the sun had risen and joined with the cool breezy weather to give the day a perfect atmosphere for tropical celebration. The day was a lovely beautiful bride. Everyone absorbed the feel of it.

Obaedo was the last child of her mother, Olohigbe, and the last also of her father. Although Obaedo's mother was the third wife, Obaedo's relationship with the two other wives and their children was very healthy. One would never know they were her step mothers. She was her mother's third of two boys and herself. On this day, Obaedo was dressed in a dark blue lady's suit, specially made for the occasion and with her well-groomed hair, it gave her the air of a little princess as she sat down there on her chair. She was with the other graduating students in a special row of seats reserved for them and calm as ever, she was with her soft feminine eyes, exchanging pleasantries. The hall was decorated to taste and classical music rose and fell in a crescendo in the background.

A beautiful practical speech on "Facing Life's Challenges with Love for Hard Work" was given by the school principal, Dr Igbinosa Afe, a close friend of Obaedo's father. The ceremony's special guest of honour, was the state Commissioner of Education, Chief Famous Edeniyere, a large sturdy man, known for very populist and colourful acts. Rumour abound that he indulges in back hand financial dealings. This he strenuously denies.

"I was not a poor man when I became a commissioner," he would say to probing questions from members of the Press. This is true. He had a vast plantation of palm trees and his commercial transport company, SAVANNAH TRAILS, was one of the favourite of passengers, travelling to Lagos from Benin City and back. A prominent member of We The People, the ruling party, he can move an audience to frenzy with impromptu speeches. During his confirmation hearings at the state House of Assembly, he had moved the legislators with his flamboyant elaboration of his agenda to boost educational opportunities for citizens of the state, through opening more universities and technical schools, increasing access to education for all with moderate fees. Today, he was dressed in an immaculate white suit, with a white bowler hat. He came with his identical twins daughters whom many in the gathering had never seen so close up before, only on television. They were really beautiful to look upon like a basket of ripe fruits.

Chief Edeniyere gave few remarks and announced that he will give the best boy and best girl, a cash donation of N20,000 naira each. The hall erupted in shouts of "Lion!", his political nickname. He seemed to enjoy the response from the crowd. After the lavish refreshment was served guests, parents and the students passing out, then came the award of excellence to deserving students. Of the many awards given out for achievement in various subjects and fields of endeavours, Obaedo won four. The most awards of the day was collected by a boy, who had been Obaedo's longtime acquaintance throughout their secondary school days, Billy Onwundinjo. He won seven awards including Best History, Best Government and Best Geography Student Award. He also won the principal's price for 'Most Intelligent Student'. Obaedo won the 'Best English' and 'Best Literature' student awards as well as the 'Most Effective School Prefect' award as the Prefect for Punctuality. Everyone knew how she was always the first in school each day and organized the school assembly.

When it was finally announced, Billy and Obaedo won the award for the Best Behaved Boy and Girl respectively. The hall erupted in cheers. Chief Edeniyere stepped forward and his aide opened his briefcase. He took out mint crisp notes and redeemed his pledge. Chief Ahamioje and his wives left their seats, danced to the front to congratulate Obaedo. Billy's parents also came to the front to thank the Education commissioner for his magnanimity.

"Don't mention, do not mention it", he said, leaving the hall to cheers of the gathered crowd.

Chapter 2
A Unique Presence.

Obaikhedo Emily Ahamioje, has always been a bright child. Prior to her entrance into primary school, her knack for asking intelligent questions and insight into things amazed many. By the time she entered school at five years old, she was ready for quality education. She had always been a pretty girl and was a spitting image of her mother but took her father's calm and disciplinary trait. Very studious and acting very mature, she exudes cleanliness and was a rallying point of several students including her class mates and junior students in her primary school and all through her secondary school. She was known to give out little gifts to junior female students in Edokpolor Grammar School just to encourage them.

Her father Chief Ahamioje had retired as a senior permanent secretary in the state civil service. He was a prominent face during years of military rule as most military governors found him very bright to work with. It is said that while several of his colleagues indulged in outright corrupt practices and employing smart ways to cover up their tracks, he made his wealth from appreciation gifts which government contractors gave him for transparently dealing with them. He was not known to demand for outright kickback and a certain percentage of the contract sum before he would help. He acted honestly and expeditiously on the files and passed honest advice on to the military governors for approval. He had once exposed a Chinese company which instead of supplying standard overhead water tanks in a water borehole project contract for many state schools brought in very substandard ones. The company also used poor iron materials for the water tanks scaffold.

"My daughter can be a victim if one of these useless things collapse on the students. Can you do this rubbish in your country? You no doubt think that we are fools over here to be played. This is our country not yours.", he had said reprimanding Qin Lin, the company's MD. It was said he turned down millions of naira to keep quiet and approve the job done. In cancelling the entire contract, the military governor had praised chief Ahamioje for his exemplary conduct in declining approval for a bad job even though he himself had been duly given a certain percentage by the company. After his retirement, chief Ahamioje became a very successful businessman setting up several gas stations across the state. He had started business with a sawmill and then branched into mechanized farming and poultry business. His keenness for education manifested in his efforts to have all his children educated. He was very eager to have them study their books not just to pass their examinations but to be well versed in the subjects. He never shied from using the whip when some of his children had made low grades. His efforts paid off as he eventually had among his children, professionals; two medical doctors, three lawyers; two accountants and an engineer.

Obaedo's success through her primary and secondary school had been a source of great joy to her father. When she won the state junior debating competition in her Junior Secondary School 3, he bought her special new clothes and accessories. Obaedo is of the type of girls who take things they do seriously yet never bear the mien of being over-serious. She carries an easy smile, is witty and rarely demonstrating her anger, has this unique presence that can make others do the right things. In her is this power of influence to move people to do things, not by playing a dominating female but by a certain liveliness. She can be real nice.

Obaedo had gained admission into secondary school on the same day with William 'Billy' Onwundinjo. Billy was the son of a Baptist preacher from Okpanam near Asaba, that ancient town separated by the river Niger from the great eastern city of Onitsha. Okpanam, with its countryside peaceful atmosphere is the home town of the late Major Chukwuma Kaduna Nzeogwu, the young idealist military officer who intervened by a military coup six years into independence to halt Nigeria's political drift, needlessly caused by politicians. Billy and Obaedo became close and excelled the most in their classes.

Chapter 3
Snack on The table.

Billy and Obaedo were seen as the pace setters in their class right from Junior Secondary 1. They asked the most intriguing questions of their teachers and volunteered answers to questions easily. They alternated the first and second positions throughout their years in secondary school. They would sometimes stay behind after school hours to read in the school library instead of dashing home like most other students. While in the library, they would do their homework, read, and sometimes, read other books that just caught their interest. Billy liked government and history a lot while Obaedo was very fond of English and Literature, especially Shakespeare. Going home, Obaedo would sometimes recite by heart the words of William Shakespeare to the thrill of Billy. She was especially fond of these lines from Macbeth:

"Tomorrow, and tomorrow, and tomorrow, creeps in this petty pace from day to day

To the last syllable of recorded time,

And all our yesterdays have lighted fools

The way to dusty death. Out, out, brief candle!

Life's but a walking shadow, a poor player

That struts and frets his hour upon the stage

And then is heard no more: It is a tale

Told by an idiot, full of sound and fury,

Signifying nothing."

Billy regaled her with the lives and deeds of nations and past presidents especially those of the United States of America and other world events. He was particularly enamored by the life of Major Chukwuma Kaduna Nzeogwu, who lived a most spartan and disciplined life. He believed that Major Nzeogwu's penchant for orderliness led him to lead Nigeria's first military coup d'etat to clean up the Augean stable and start a practically new nation. He often recited to Obaedo, portions of the speech the young Major gave on January 15, 1966. Sometimes just to make Obaedo laugh, he would mix up Major Nzeogwu's speech:

"In the name of the Supreme Council of the Nigerian Armed Forces, I, Major Billy Onwundinjo, hereby declare martial law over all provinces of Nigeria. The constitution is suspended and all schools are closed down until further notice. All political, cultural, tribal and trade union activities, together with all demonstrations and unauthorized gatherings, excluding worship, are banned until further notice. The aim of the Revolutionary Council is to establish a strong, united and prosperous nation, free from corruption and internal strife.

Our method of achieving this is strictly military but Obaedo Ahamioje will become the new prime minister to run the affairs of government."

As time went on, petty rumours began to spread about them from other students. After finishing from the library they would stroll home together. While Obaedo's family home was closer to the school, Billy's was further down, off the main street. Once, during lunch break in their Junior Secondary 3, Billy stayed back in class reading a cartoon book while most of the students had gone out to buy snacks and play football. As the lunch break was drawing to a close and students started returning to class, Obaedo strolled in with an egg roll snack which she purchased for Billy and dropped it on his desk with an ice cream. The other boys murmured loudly.

"But she is only doing her job as a good wife.", said a rough-looking boy with a dirty face, Ero.

The class burst out laughing. Some girls started mouthing things, mocking Obaedo. She just sat on her seat, unruffled. Ero had once told the class that he had seen both of them holding hands going home together. It turned out not to be true. They had actually bought a roasted corn on their way back home and Ero saw them holding to it trying to break it into two. Billy would hear all these insinuations but would show no emotion.

Billy was comfortable being in Obaedo's company. Her inquisitive mind and mental alertness pleased him a lot. She could reason out their school work when they tried to do their homework. Apart from this, Obaedo was never quarrelsome, loud or bossy. These were flaws that he had observed in the character of several girls in school. He despised these traits in women. Obaedo was a different kind. A vivacious girl that was yet calm with a certain tenderness and compassion. Her ideas were always brilliant and her beauty enhances her. He thought he liked her a lot.

Chapter 4
Clean Ways.

Even among Obaedo's family, the talk of her friendship with Billy was known. They perceived it as a healthy relationship between two studious students, giving no other interpretation to it. Once when he visited her home as he often did, her father was around with his friend and family physician, the elderly Dr. James Iruedo. Dr. Iruedo was a leading general practice medical practitioner who had once served as Chief Medical director of the state's General Hospital and as state commissioner of health. He had been appointed as Chief Medical Director following a riot that broke out on the death of a patient through negligence in the state hospital. The patient, an accident victim was rushed to the hospital but no doctor was on ground. Those who brought the woman had been made to deposit some amount of money even before anything could be done. Despite pleas, the scornful nurses had stood their grounds. When the doctor finally came and ordered for an X-Ray, the films were finished in the store and he then directed that the patient be transferred to the University of Benin Teaching Hospital, several kilometers away. By then the woman had died. As news spread, concerned people gathered at the hospital and before long, fire has been set to some hospital offices. The government later carried out a purge of top hospital personnel and appointed Dr. Iruedo to head the hospital. He wasted no time in using the prevalent mood in the state to order for brand new hospital equipment and to employ more doctors and nurses. From Chief Medical Director, he was made Commissioner of Health from where he revolutionized health care delivery in the state. He introduced mandatory practical course test on ethics and civility for all hospital staff which they had to pass and made famous an employment policy, 'Only Employing Smiling Nurses'. One remarkable achievement of his was to open new cottage hospitals in rural areas with a doctor and a health educationist stationed there. He also banned mobile commercial sellers of drugs saying that they cannot be trusted and made traditional herbal medicine practitioners to be screened and registered. When he had retired from government employment, he established his own private hospital, Oasis, which out-ranked the state hospital in infrastructure, equipment and service delivery. He is known to pay his workers very well and on time too. He always referred to his workers as his assets.

"Hah, young man. How is your education going?"

"Very well sir."

"I know. Your friend went on an errand for me. She will soon be back."

"Okay sir."

The doctor was gazing directly into Billy's eyes. "Do you play football in school?" he inquired from Billy.

"Not always sir. Most of the boys play rough and I try to avoid it."

"I thought so too. Maybe you will be better off in athletics then. There is no much contact. As a young man you should take active part in sporting activities."

Chief Ahamiojie cut in, "He loves table tennis a lot. I think he came to play with his friend as well as help her wash her clothes." They all burst out laughing.

Obaedo's father's home was a large compound close to the Ikpoba riverside in Upper Lawani Street of Benin City. The area was particularly serene with a pristine peace. From the house one can see over the river, the other side, the Ikpoba hill area of the city which leads to the eastern part of the country. To view the face of the slow moving water of the Ikpoba River was a delight. Many loved to inhale its scent and it was a popular resort for young children and adults to come swim in and wash their clothes. It is a beautiful breathtaking landscape with the gentle breeze strolling out from the river enveloping the vicinity in its embrace. Billy often would go visit Obaedo and from the balcony they would survey with their eyes the beautiful landscape, the slow running waters of the river and the area across, especially the vehicles climbing up and coming down the Ikpoba hill road. They would also see different customers entering and going out from Mama Onome's pepper soup Joint. An Urhobo woman from near Sapele in the Niger Delta, Mama Onome lived close to the river and has a very popular pepper soup Joint where she sold fresh palm wine and fresh fish pepper soup from fish caught from the river. She would set her nets late at night and wake up early in the morning to draw them out. Very hardworking, her husband a renowned quarellsome drunkard, Orogun Otite, had left her to marry a younger Urhobo girl who had a thriving hair dressing salon. Mama Onome had continued alone to train Onome and her other children in school. There were days when Obaedo's father made special order of her fresh fish pepper soup for his guests.

One remarkable day Billy had visited Obaedo's house was when she was preparing to represent the school in the state junior secondary debating competition. Billy had represented the school in the quiz contest and won the state junior award. Now was the debate season. On this Saturday, while Billy sat down and acted as the panel, Obaedo faced him and would repeat the convincing lines she intended to use against her opponent. The topic was "Indiscipline in Schools: Who to Blame, Parents or Teachers?" Obaedo was expected to argue for parents to be held accountable.

'The Bible is God's eternal wisdom for men of all ages and He expressly told us when there were no schools yet that, "The rod and reproof give wisdom: but a child left to himself bringeth his mother to shame". Proverbs 29:15. God Almighty was basically talking to parents here. The rod, physical discipline; reproof, strong scolding with words. This is a parents' duty prescribed by the Head parent of all men. Distinguished members of the panel, my name is Obaedo Ahamioje and I am here to…'

They continued from noon until evening in her father's living room. Obaedo's mum sometimes came in to see them exchanging views and she would make suggestions. She prepared for them a lovely dish of rice, chicken stew and fried plantain, which was Billy's favourite. After the rehearsals, they ate together and Obaedo walked Billy down the road a bit as he went home. On their way, they saw Mallam Ali the *Suya* meat seller preparing his delicacies for the night. They also met Ero, their noisy classmate. Smiling mischievously, he asked Billy if he went to Obaedo's house to pay her bride price. Billy smiled and they walked on. As they did, Obaedo thanked Billy for his help through school and on this very day for the oncoming debate. He merely shrugged, giving the impression that he had enjoyed it all.

"You treat me like I am amazing. Why?", Obaedo asked.

"But you are amazing."

"No, I am Obaedo."

"I think you deserve all the help you can get. You like to excel."

"I feel like I can tell you anything. I see a rainbow in your eyes", Obaedo said coyly

"Say this again so Ero and Osaro can hear you.", Billy replied laughing.

"Let them hear."

Infact, Obaedo had once scribbled a note to Billy in class which Osaro had snatched and read out. The whole class had erupted. The note was written on a day their teachers were in a staff meeting and most subjects were not being taught.
'I like your genuine gentleness and your clean ways.' the note said.

Everyone knew of Billy Onwundinjo's clean ways. On that very day, while a boy in their class had angrily confronted Obaedo about her admonishing his younger brother on his dirty school uniform, Billy had stepped in and defused the situation amicably.

"It is just her care and concern that made her tell him to improve on his cleanliness. That shouldn't make you angry," Billy told Ogie.

His handling of the situation had awakened deep feminine feelings in her. He was her undeniable attraction.

Billy was the fifth child of his parents. His father was the pastor of the city Baptist church. A very pious man, he was known for his strict adherence to the Scriptures in his sermons. Once, he delivered the sermon at the Armed Forces

Remembrance Day and he used the words of John the Baptist in admonishing soldiers. He read *Luke 3: 14 And the soldiers likewise demanded of him, saying, And what shall we do? And he said unto them, Do violence to no man, neither accuse any falsely; and be content with your wages.*

He then called out, "Soldiers!"

Not getting the response he wanted, he repeated, "Answer me soldiers of the nation!"

A roar went out. The military governor of the state, Col. Yakubu Malumfashi and other dignitaries were in attendance.

"God said you shouldn't be seen beating your wives or civilians like they are animals. Answer me!"

They chorused back, "Yes sir!"

"God said don't go putting false lying accusations on people and you must live only with the pay you get from government. Is God's Word true?"

They chorused back.

The place was electrified.

In his church, he would preach his sermons with lively examples from the Bible. He would often say that the

Holy Bible is God's entire thoughts to mankind and that if anything was not in the Bible, men ought to stay away from it. An avid student of Martin Luther's writings, he believed like Luther that God has preserved the experience of salvation and holiness by means of a Book, the Bible and not in the shifting ecstasies of men's minds and their religious ecclesiastical councils. To him, God's given Word is fixed, unchanging and not to be put on a spin nor to be privately re-interpreted. It is straightforward and means exactly what it says. He believed that real men of God will be subservient to the Scriptures. Growing up under his parents had helped Billy a lot. His earliest memories as a child were of being woken up early each morning to attend their family altar prayers, where his father would read small portions of Scriptures out of a big Bible in their living room. After exhorting them, he would pray with his family. That was how their day started each day of the week. This family tradition has continued on. His parents' calm and easy going life style had influenced him in terms of being so disciplined and calm. Never one to indulge in a shouting match with his school mates, he was especially reserved but friendly. He avoided the company of known rough boys in school who were known for bad jokes, rough looks and immoral behaviours and remained committed to his books. He had seen in Obaedo some things about himself. He saw that seriousness of a student that he was and thought she was a disciplined and well brought up girl.

Billy had been chosen to give a talk about Christmas in their school's last Christmas carol night. Quoting extensively from the Bible, he presented Christ birth in a most revealing way to show how the world needed a Messiah.

'And when He was finally born, angels sang out. And why can't we all sing out tonight too'

Everyone then joined the choir in singing *"Silent Night."*

Their principal was so impressed. 'That was great Billy'. 'Thank you sir.'

After the ceremony, Obaedo walked up to Billy. The look in her eyes told him that she was impressed.

Chapter 5
Charisma.

Obaedo's father was an Anglican by Christian faith. His family attended church services mostly on Sundays. Obaedo's elder brother Johnson had on entering the University of Benin to study medicine, found a group of Christians on campus. Looking always well dressed and bonding together as brethren, he discovered that they were a sort of offshoot of the Pentecostal Church Christians. Their services were not formal and they talked about their church ministry with zeal. Infact their Christianity revolved around their church and the church founder. This church was founded by a very charismatic Bishop who spoke fluently and boldly.

Bishop Emmanuel Ifenacho Azuka was a fatherly figure, robust, large and very convincing in his speech. Known to preach with lively demonstrations, he had the charisma of a typical black American preacher and enjoyed the active feedback from his audience to his sermons. He made claims of being an apostle in the mode of the original Disciples of Christ. His church was large with hundreds of believers. Total submission is required from its followers to the Church leadership. Infact it is often gossiped that you don't sin against God while under the Bishop; you sin against him and his Church. And for that, you will be heavily lambasted and wounded with words beyond measure. An erring member can be so ostracized and they'll do pretty much everything in their power to Make life hell if the member doesn't bend quickly and go acquiescing. The students in the university campus who attended his church were very zealous towards this church and went to services there on Wednesdays evening and Sundays.

Emmanuel Azuka had lived in Benin City as a businessman before the Nigerian Civil War Hailing from the core East across the River Niger, he had moved down to Benin City after Nigeria gained her independence in 1960. He became successful as a provisions and cosmetics goods businessman owning chains of shops in retail and wholesale trade. He later became a major distributor to many companies and also bought goods from Onitsha. He was also a landlord in Benin, with several properties. After the invasion of Benin City by Biafran forces on 9th August, 1967, he had a premonition that war would come into Benin City. Just before General Murtala Muhammed led federal forces entered Benin, he had moved his family away and was spared the atrocities visited upon those Igbos who had remained back in Benin. He was particularly pained to have lost several of his fellow Igbo business partners and friends who refused to flee Benin City. They were hunted down by the locals, accused of being collaborators with the Biafran troops and finished off by the northern led forces just for being Igbos. Hearing this tragic news, he had enlisted in the Biafran armed forces where he rose to become a Major.

After the war, Emmanuel Azuka came back to Benin, only to see his shops looted and his properties now occupied and claimed by the local indigenes. Broken, he began afresh in business, selling building materials for more than a decade until one day he spoke of a spiritual experience with a divine being who commissioned him to enter the ministry and preach the Word. He would usually say later that he had made it a hundred-fold in the ministry what he never made in business. He was a man who carried his calling and ministry's position into the 'enemy''s camp so to speak, proclaiming to all of how he met the divine who commissioned him. He would most times make criminally slanderous attacks on those ministers who refused to buy into his convictions and claims of being an apostle of Jesus Christ. He spared no harsh words on those who stood on their convictions that the Bishop's experiences should be subordinate to the authority of plain Scriptures and those who dismissed his ministry as the delusion of an uneducated proud man. He was wild in castigating them. And then miracles began. Signs, wonders, answered prayers, attended his ministry and its fame spread rapidly not just among the ignorant and credulous alone, it was supported by professionals and preachers who came to identify with him. It baffled some however how this ministry with its apparent absurdity could attract so many intelligent people across the country and beyond. In reality, many of those who devoutly follow him are actually productive and healthy individuals who are successful in mainstream society. But the Bishop had been able to engage them with his charisma and the power of his voice. They were also attracted because of their inner love for deeper truths which his ministry claimed to have. They wanted to belong to an organization that seemingly had their Christian teachings and ways more classy than others. It would appear that the spiritual complacency of a people and their almost childish belief in anyone that mounts the podium with a microphone in his hand and speaks fluently, even with so slender a fountain of Biblical authority, can sway most people. Men's propensity for hearing new and exciting things gave the Bishop a harvest of members. He had managed to convince many that hidden truths were being revealed to him for the first time ever and he did this by a perfect blend of truth and fiction which he seemed an expert at. None dared question if he was a prophet, to whom the Word of the Lord Biblically came, considering his lofty claims. But as always, his charisma was engulfing even though any sincere observer would plainly see that the man was a distorter and a defiler of the Word.

Bishop Azuka's wife was the self-effacing Chinelo, the daughter of his father's friend. Having known themselves for many years and being close friends, he had married her before the civil war. Meek and caring, she had stayed with him through thick and thin. Their union was blessed with five children; the first a girl, Ifeyinwa; then three boys, Nduka, Onuora and Ibe; and then a girl, Ijeoma. Ifeyinwa was a graduate of Public Administration from the University of

Benin. She dresses nicely always according to trendy fashion, with a super confidence and a strong feminine personality. Exhibiting sexual charms, very few men could look upon her without admiration. She is however filled with that lust for authority and power which is generally sought for by men. Tall and fair-complexioned, she carries herself like a goddess, making a religion of her self-worth. She got married to a successful engineer, an Igbo Christian brother in their church, Dubem Onwuatuegwu, who had relocated from Northern Nigeria because of constant religious riots and upheavals that leads to the shedding of blood of innocent southern lives. Dubem set up his civil engineering firm in Benin and was patronized by government and private firms. He became very fervent in the Bishop's church. Many still believe that Ifeyinwa had agreed to marry him because of his wealth. The marriage however did not last long as talk of frequent quarrels spread. It became known that being the daughter of Bishop Azuka got into her head and she went domineering, trying to boss her husband at home and in family decisions. She could stay away from her matrimonial home at her father's for up to a week sometimes and her husband would be all alone and lonely. Not wanting to enter into servitude in his own house, he sought to impose his will rather than suffer from being weak and vacillating.

Bishop Azuka naturally took sides with his daughter and he sternly rebuked her husband in church one Sunday. On getting home, when Ifeyinwa instead of pacifying him for the open disgrace tried to rub things in, being frustrated and disappointed, he gave her a sound beating and kicked her out of his house. She settled into her father's house from where she won the nasty custody battle for their only daughter.

Ifeyinwa ran her father's church administration and could be real brash and haughty, a contrast to her mother who avoided the limelight. Although not a deacon, she was the de facto head deacon and cast a heavy influence on all departments of the church. It is known that she approves all special songs sung by the choir. Ifeyinwa was also over couples intending to get married. Although she ran it as a tight ship, she ran it well. Those wanting to get married had to go through her controlled phases. If a brother is seen on his own talking to a sister for more than a few minutes at a time, he had better be ready to explain himself to Ifeyinwa for he can be in real trouble. Phase one is simply just talking to the sister with her permission. He talks to her and if he likes her, he will tell Ifeyinwa that he wants to get to know the sister better. All these are officially in the first phase. Before this first phase you are not allowed to relate to that specific sister and that is it. Phase two is when they are allowed to go outings together but no touching or hand holding. Phase three is engagement where the brother has to ask the woman's father for his permission to marry, and then propose. By her rules, they cannot kiss before their wedding day. However in practice most couples end up sneaking kisses and some even get into penetrative sex. Before a couple are engaged, they both have to meet with the Bishop and his daughter where they confess any sexual activity they ever indulged in from youth. It is nicknamed the 'Heat Room', because of the tension intending couples face there revealing sordid details of their past. One sister, Ndidi after confessing her past to the Bishop felt so embarrassed and drained of self-confidence and she left the Church without going ahead with the marriage. Rumour later spread, ostensibly leaked by Ifeyinwa, of the sordid things that Ndidi had confessed. It was said that she confessed that she constantly had made romantic and sexual advances towards men for years; she kissed a boy in her Primary 5; holding hands, giving hugs and touching the genitals of his boss and then details of her sexual deviancy. Sister Ndidi later told people that as she made her past known that the Bishop seemed to be relishing it all. She wondered how she could ever be under him when he had known her so exposed. Ifeyinwa throwing back on Ndidi was once heard saying how a sister so rotten could ever have made a successful wife. Ndidi later got married to the local branch manager of Tropics Bank, Jideofor Ogbonnaya.

Some sisters, who naturally were not approached by the brother of their choice and getting 'old', agreed to marry a brother in whom they were not fully interested and who wasn't really in their class. Feeling left out of being among the married in Church and the fear that they would lose out to produce their own children, they agreed to marry. Sister Nebu's case is remarkable. A successful lawyer, after the couple said their vows and it came time to kiss for the first time at the altar, she cringed after one peck and pushed her husband, a school teacher, away.

Ifeyinwa also had a firm control over the young people. They often joked that she monitors what time they wake up, to how they dress, to how to wipe their....Her controlling nature can make the place for them some time to feel like a prison camp and some who couldn't take it, had left the church.

The three boys of Bishop Azuka are all graduates but unlike Nduka who went into business, the other two are civil servants and are active in their father's church as players of musical instruments.

The last child of the Bishop, Ijeoma, is an undergraduate studying History at the University of Benin. She is known to do nothing scandalous by halves. With a long and crafty-looking face, she is full of a pathological aggression and rarely attends church services. She is as ugly as she is loose and can be real saucy. Dismissed by many as decadent, there is much attempt to conceal her sexual wantonness by the façade of getting her to sing special songs in church sometimes but her lewdness as a minister's daughter is second to none.

Obaedo's brother, Johnson, started attending the

services of this church. Obaedo during visits to his brother at his hostel, would see some of the Bishop's sermon books and would read some. She found them interesting. Their father had dismissed the Bishop as another chariot chaser and showed no interest in his ministration on television. He was particularly critical of most modern day churches who according to him were charlatans, merely materialistic wealth-chasers, bent on only seeing the destruction of their enemies.

"If you want wealth, go and work hard and consistently. Don't stay in your house or church praying. You are an idle and lazy thief. The Bible condemns idleness and slothfulness. Even the great apostle Paul, who was so vindicated and backed by God Almighty as His servant and who said 'follow me as I follow Christ', had to work, making tents to survive. Don't mind these charlatans." He would tell his physician.

"Jesus Christ was the humblest of men, so meek and retiring. But these so-called leaders of today want to be renown, celebrated and worshipped. Always seeking fleshy publicity. Why? How can these people claim to be followers of Christ and are always pronouncing curses upon their enemies. Christ said to love your enemies. I just don't get the contradiction. I don't want my enemies to die, I want them to live and see what God will do for me and perhaps they too will repent and be blessed by God. David said in the Psalms, 'Thou preparest a table before me in the presence of mine enemies.' In their presence. As long as I am trying to serve my God, I cannot be obsessed with being afraid that somebody using charms will kill me or harm my family. If it is my Father's will for them to end my life, I go Home to be with Him. I cannot live with looking over my shoulders, placing curses on imaginary enemies."

Chief Ahamioje's religious convictions had been fortified from teaching by his late father, his own experiences in life and lately from revulsion at what he had termed the commercialisation of God. When therefore as part of activities to mark Dr. Iruedo's 70th birthday, his children had arranged a special public lecture in his honour, delivered by the Head of Religious Studies of the University of Lagos, Professor Ola Oni, Chief Ahamioje was on the side of those who praised the lecture that day. The lecture attracted leading clergy men, the cream of society and top government officials. Professor Oni chose the topic, 'Nigeria, Our Successful Men, Our Economy, Our Christianity', and stirred up the hornet's nest. Infact his lecture was the talk of the town for several weeks.

"Corruption and incompetence are the hallmark of Nigeria's years of independence from Britain. With this under-delivering of economic progress to Nigerians and the people therefore reduced to slave-like struggles for survival, yearning for the good life; then entered preachers, masters of the spin on the Word of God, who deliver smooth-talking prosperity-laced Gospel for the better life. Thousands of Nigerians fell for it. This brand of Christianity in Nigeria was spearheaded right from this city from the early 1980s as economic hardship started kicking in. As the civilian leadership of the early 1980s toiled with the country's economy and then the military-backed Structural Adjustment Programme came on board, industries collapsed, hundreds of thousands lost their jobs. Getting businesses to thrive and getting good government jobs became very competitive. Then churches mainly of the Pentecostal stock, saw an opening to exploit the vulnerabilities of millions by goading them towards a form of Christianity where God and indeed church becomes an avenue to get wealthy and to live the better life, to enjoy prosperity. They pushed aside plain Scriptures that taught that Christianity is about Cross-bearing and striving to live the Life of the Christ, most times going through trials. These trendy preachers held out church to the economically crushed people as a way out of all suffering, a way to make it in life. They came offering commercial-laced colourful prayers to defeat ones' enemies. And in a society where superstitious beliefs and savage wickedness still thrive, people, anybody, will want this. The trap was set."

A low murmur swept through the audience.

"These preachers turned the God of the Bible, a Holy and Sacred Being, into a sort of genie, where men can use God, infact command Him to deliver all they want. So instead of conforming to the Will of the Savior, to His Word, Christians are edged on to impose their desires and will on God and He MUST meet it. Just like the ways of untrained bastard children.

These preachers were filled with lust for power, popularity and wealth. They wanted earthly glory; to be looked up to and to control the lives of people. The very opposite of Jesus Christ. Playing on the peoples' wants and needs, with twisted promises from the Word of God to banish poverty forever; miracles and signs became the primary task of churches not the commission to build lives for Heaven. Preachers presented the church as a sort of God's cashier for men's needs. Naturally, all sorts, especially unconverted people filled the pews and church membership blossomed. And this is taken as church growing.

And seeing the trendy new lives of these pastors, how they were 'making it'," the audience burst out laughing. The face of a leading Bishop in the state was a mask of anger. The professor continued.

"And seeing the trendy new lives of these pastors, how they were 'making it', thousands more entered Bible schools to get a basic background to start pastorial work. Others still didn't need to go that extent of Bible school; they just opened shop and started their own churches, their own business.

Not openly known was that unsaved pagans, cultists and evil occultists joined in this race and with clear demonic powers and influences, also opened their own churches, working miracles, having prosperity and "deliverance" results. Today, the most visible structures on Nigeria streets are churches; ranging from the decrepit small store to the mega sized auditoriums that hold thousands every service. Business is booming.

In all these, real godly Biblical Christianity have been pushed aside and a new Jesus, a new Gospel wherein Christians pursue wealth as a major goal; where looking out for and praying death upon their enemies is the vogue. Infact this generation of Christians don't care if they are just as badly behaved and immorally behaved as the world they are supposed to show the light to. Just as long as they prosper and hear prophecies. They can go into politics and steal as much as the non-believers. The only difference is their going to church.

By the time one of the forerunners of this kind of end time Christianity suddenly died, his family inherited his huge wealth and investments and became the new overlords of their church organisation. The modern Christians, they don't care about this shamelessness. As long as they get results and money is pouring in. They put words in God's mouth and deceive the people. And the people shout in excitement, 'Hallelujah! We are getting results'. People are whipped into a frenzy just only to get miracles and blessings from God Almighty. The ostentatiously dressed preachers in bright gaudy clothes, use voice accentuations and manipulation expertly to railroad the people on."

The audience clapped.

"Physical poverty in Nigeria has not decreased. But these preachers-entrepreneurs...", his words were drown out by the loud rumble from the audience. Professor Oni waited for calm to be restored and continued with his barrage.

"These preachers-entrepreneurs and their families are in a stupendous bounty of wealth, investments and glory. Many of these Nigerian pastors are now listed among the richest in the world, even though the citizens of this country are still plagued by stark poverty and crime. From owing thousands of church branches which turn up money into their coffers; owing fleet of cars; private jets; jewelries, the void left by a true Nigeria leadership to lift the nation, has been taken over by these fabulously wealthy, smooth talking deceivers. The Church has turned people into victims of materialism under the guise of prosperity. Yes, they get the results that people so badly crave because of a collapsed economy. Nigerians want to worship. It is natural to men. They also want the good life. Nothing is wrong with that at all. A thriving economy and then hard work like that of our distinguished Dr. Iruedo can bring that. It is not dependent upon church at all. But these trendy preachers come using God to manipulate the people. They come all enthused and the people are so carried away. The people love this new feel. They pack the churches full where they are not told to straighten up their lives. The people are not sternly told that stealing public funds, defrauding their business partners, indulging in 419, being slothful and lazy are sins. Church going is not at all to major on godly living and to shun social vices, drunkenness, fornication, adultery, female trafficking themselves to Italy for commercial sex, but they are told all their desires will be met by an Almighty God whose only job has become to provide prosperity for men and destroy their enemies. End time Christianity.

These preachers quote the words of Deuteronomy 28: 13 *And the LORD shall make thee the head, and not the tail; and thou shalt be above only, and thou shalt not be beneath;*

But they craftily ignore the other part of that same verse and the next verses:

IF that thou hearken unto the commandments of the LORD thy God, which I command thee this day, to observe and to do them: 14 And thou shalt not go aside from any of the words which I command thee this day, to the right hand, or to the left, to go after other gods to serve them. 15 ¶ But it shall come to pass, if thou wilt not hearken unto the voice of the LORD thy God, to observe to do all his commandments and his statutes which I command thee this day; that all these curses shall come upon thee, and overtake thee:

They conveniently, trickily ignore that God based His blessing His own people, {not everybody} IF only they keep obeying Him. And God promised curses if they ever stop. But this new Gospel tells you God will keep blessing you regardless what you do. And millions of prosperity-seeking but unsaved Nigerians flock into these sanctuaries of prosperity, until criminals and the devilishly wicked have made church their second home. Yet the Jehovah of the Bible is watching all this filth. The same God who destroyed His chosen people Israel when they turned from His Word is still alife. So this new Christianity comes, highly colourful and flamboyant, crowd-pulling, pushing men to set their hearts on carnal glory. And millions fall for it. People have been twisted to go attain the kind of wealth and prosperity that the church was not promised in God's Word to provide. They have been lured to go seeking a God Who will provide everything they need without them living fully totally by His Word. That kind of Christianity is sweet but it is not what is promised in God's Holy Word."

By the time he finished, the greater part of the audience were on their feet cheering. Some Bishops surrounded by their armed anti-riot police escorts, had walked out during the lecture, got into their flashy cars and drove off with their convoy. One Bishop, Peter Amadasun was seen outside pouring invectives on Professor Oni. Chief Ahamioje who was chosen to give the vote of thanks, was overtly elated and thanked the professor profusely for his boldness and clarity of thought.

On passing out from secondary school, Obaedo went to live with her elder brother who had finished his medical programme and was doing his internship at the University of Benin Teaching Hospital, UBTH. He had been given a very decent apartment at the Doctors' Quarters. After having earlier read some of his brother's church books, she saw no reason for not following him to their church on Sunday.

On her first visit, she was impressed with the atmosphere at the church and the well-dressed people. The music was good and the singing session of the service was long, soothing and classy. It was led by the Bishop's son, Nduka, who also conducted the choir. The congregational singing, handclapping and dancing was energetic and infectious. Special songs were sung by two elegantly dressed sisters and then the large choir. It was moving.

Then came the Bishop with his sermon on, God Called Men. Humility was not his thing. He conveyed too much the image of a preeminent authoritarian for a preacher. His speaking was forceful yet alluring. Dressed in an expensive black suit with a white shirt and matching tie, he cut the figure of a top government personnel. In his sermon, he traced a long line of men in the Bible and in church history whom God used to trigger a Move or revival in their time and to whom the people gave total heed. He emphasized 'total heed'. The audience was held by his presence of authority, a magnetism of mystery and his message. He was most effective in exercising an authority to their inner man, their emotional center. Concluding, he drew a black picture of the Christianity of the present day and said that God won't fail to have a witness to raise a standard again in this day. His pulpit display was very moving. The congregation erupted in frenzy, people were convulsed in ecstasy on his sermon and some were falling all about the place. Melodious playing of the piano filled the church and the atmosphere was drenched in its intensity. Many worshippers were crying out and praying. When the service was over, all were ushered out seat by seat. Obaedo was thrilled to have attended the service. Her brother never wanting to push, didn't ask her about the service but he enjoyed reading her mood. To him, she had seen the truth and would certainly belong here and leave their old family church.

Just before they drove out, the Bishop's son Nduka, came to greet Obaedo's brother, calling him "Doc".

"Meet my sister, Obaedo."

Nduka took her hand and said "I know. Same face. How was the service?"

She gave a nod in affirmation, to which he replied,

"Come back again and we'll be glad to have you in the choir."

To this Obaedo smiled but her brother laughed and asked, "Do you know if she can sing?"

"I will teach her"

As they drove home, an impressed Obaedo was looking forward to telling Billy about her experience with these people.

Chapter 6
Testing the Waters.

When the Joint Admissions and Matriculation Board, JAMB, examinations results were released on 19 December 1999, Obaedo had scored above the cut-off mark to gain admission to study English, Literature and Classics at the University of Benin. Billy was also admitted to study Law. On that day, Nigerian President Olusegun Obasanjo had ordered the Nigerian Armed Forces to raid the town of Odi in the Niger Delta, in response to the murder of twelve policemen by local militants. The total destruction of the town with attendant loss of lives later gripped the nation and many would see it as the main catalyst for the future restiveness and militancy that over whelmed the oil-rich Niger Delta. Chief Ahamioje was particularly touched by such an incident taking place under a civilian administration.

The Matriculation ceremony of Billy and Obaedo took place in January 2000. It was a very colourful event. Obaedo's father came with food and drinks which were served to their invited guests and well-wishing passers-by. One shock they experienced early in university was during the orientation ceremony by their combined faculties' students associations for new students, with one of the events being a beauty pageant show for new female students. Obaedo, who had predictably ignored pleas to take part, had to leave the event with Billy as they couldn't bear watching innocent and naïve new female students parade the podium, adorning scandalous provocative dresses, drawing cat calls from males in spasms of pure unadulterated lust. They quickly discovered that a university can be a place of freedom without responsibility. Young men and women are easily carried away by this. They saw how easily young men and girls from respectable backgrounds turned coarse and decadent. Some male students particularly put up very bad attitude, displaying animal-like aggression. They would learn later of the untouchables; boys who were kingpins of secret cult groups and who had rich and powerful backers in society. They discovered that many students including those in Christian groups easily got into furtive relationships that tended towards fornication. Infact fornication is the rule rather than the exception on campus. It is like a plague. Some of the males from not-too-wealthy parents, unexplainably would elect to go hungry just to meet the needs of their trendy girlfriends. Boys constantly got close to pretty looking girls to become friends and indulge in casual sex. The campus Christian groups had their own pastors who mostly acted like demi-gods, rarely attending lectures and were often seen in the company of the sisters. Many of these sisters frequented the off-campus apartment of these pastors to carry out chores for them and most times passed the night.

Billy had heard his father preach on the Daughters of Men from Genesis 6 in the Bible, the upsurge on the earth of beautiful and highly enticing women in the days of Noah which subsequently led to the moral collapse of that age as men inevitably became women-chasers. Now he was to see at first hand such a raw display of luscious women like never before. Everywhere you turned, there were waves of these young, highly seductive, beautiful girls accentuating their sexiness in provocative dresses and body shapes as they twisted up and down. Girls so sexy, in their early-nineties to twenties; fashionable ones, those with bleached skins, those with protruding breasts, slim ones with curves and beautiful dark hair and enticing eyes. What he saw daily was an oasis of 'hotties'. High heeled shoes are standard; short skirts and short dresses are constant. Those who have real feminine curves aren't afraid to show them off. Anytime they leave their hostel, they get dressed up for it to look their best and they usually don't wear that much either. They exude confident sexiness to the male. It's like they need to be admired and lusted after or their days/lives won't have meaning. Some would just wear jeans with no pockets to show their butt off as much as possible! However, behind their speaking in borrowed accent was their sassy attitude. Many of these girls wear such suggestive clothes to their church fellowship, to lectures and even when going to privately see lecturers in their offices. Within him, he wondered how the males could refrain from having constant bombardment of their minds with lewd thoughts seeing such open display of sexuality. Even the Christians females were not left out in portraying their seductiveness. It was like a competition amongst most all the girls. He was told that during the military rule, most times buses were sent from Government House to pick girls to attend guests at Friday night parties. These dream girls to politicians and top government officials are notably extra-beautiful looking and stand out from the rest with long curly hair, artificial hair, with make-ups and seductive hips. They can flash a smile that can light up a room; they can engage in smart and educated conversation and are as fit and athletic as a whip. Independent, humorous, warm, and passionate, they are friendly and sensual. They spend more money than others on beautifying themselves and take pride in their appearance. It's a cultural phenomenon with them and it seems it can't be stopped. It's all about beauty, elegance, and intelligence in order to decide who's the fairest of them all. Billy could only shake his head considering the plight of their parents who would think that their daughters are in the university getting an education and a moral training for life.

Obaedo and Billy settled down to their studies and continued their reading in the library after observing their afternoon siesta each school day. While Obaedo continued staying with her brother in his apartment, Billy stayed in the university hostel. As they met in the library, they would share their daily experiences about their studies and other small talk. Billy who kept an ear opened for world events would tell Obaedo of any major news that he heard on his small transistor radio. Obaedo started telling Billy how different boys in her department and elsewhere were pestering her to go out with them and how she consistently refused their advances. Once, she visited Billy's hostel to collect a General Studies textbook, a course for all new students. The eyes of Billy's roommates almost popped out. Their look certainly embarrassed her. Their brooding eyes were so intense.

After she had left, Dan, one of Billy's roommate asked him, "How is she?"

Billy knowing where he was going ignored the question. Then Kenny blurted out, "How do you expect him to know when he is gay." They all broke into fits of laughter.

As the first semester progressed, Obaedo's complaints of boys' harassment kept growing. Some simply wanted to go out with a decent girl; many others had not so pure motives. Billy would tell her to just ignore them but she knew that was becoming a stale option. One Friday, after Woke, a final year student of her department who had given her a note in class the day before to allow him buy her lunch on Saturday, she agreed. She didn't tell Billy as they read that Friday evening.

Woke did all to impress her. The son of a wealthy family from Rivers State in the Niger Delta, he was not known for womanising as most boys. He obviously was carried away by Obaedo's beauty and comportment. Obaedo did enjoy herself although she was not at ease. Something kept telling her that she ought to have told Billy. When Woke asked her for another lunch date on the following Saturday, she told him, she couldn't. She watched as the young man's mood darkened, his eyes looked pained.

"Is it because of your boyfriend?", he asked.

"He is not my boyfriend. He is just a very close friend that I cherish a lot more than a boyfriend thing. He has been my best friend and confidant. I wouldn't want to offend him nor give him up for anything."

"I wouldn't want to replace him. I just enjoy your company and how you conduct yourself."

"Thank you very much. I enjoyed it last time too. Let that be okay for now please."

As Woke walked away, Obaedo felt pity for him.

When Obaedo confided in Billy what she had done the weekend before with Woke and the situation she just handled, she was actually testing the waters to see Billy's reaction. To her, Woke was a nice guy and harmless. If she was expecting a rude answer from Billy, she would have been surprised.

"Am not really your task master Oba. You are a grown up girl and will get these offers and temptations. It becomes your decision to know which is proper and which to avoid. Although I don't think that I will enjoy seeing you with rough boys anyway. I know Woke too, he is smart. But why can he not go out with his own classmates? You are not even within his age bracket. But be careful whatever you do."

She almost broke down sobbing at his advice. She was surprised he didn't blurt out about her being now corrupt. He wasn't jealous and mad. Taking control of herself, she told him she would be really careful. Back in her room, she wondered deep inside her why Billy did not madly object to her going out with another boy. She tried to think why but just felt he was just a matured guy doing things that most boys would never condone. But he should be jealous, why is he not, she thought. Perhaps he just knows somehow that the boys wouldn't be able to move her from the path of decency. She smiled to herself.

Apart from that lunch date with Woke, she also went out with a boy in the department of Linguistics and then a young lecturer in her department who had also been pestering her for a dinner outing. She went out with him and they both had excellent discussion over dinner, the type of discussions that Obaedo liked. She told Billy after each outing and he would listen and flow along, then ask questions calmly. If he was jealous, he knew how to conceal it. But one thing, he knew was that he couldn't bottle her up. She had to decide for herself what will please her.

On March 21, 2000, Pope John Paul II had begun an official visit to Israel and just as their first semester examinations was about to commence, the non-academic staff of the university went on strike to press for their outstanding extra-work allowances to be paid. It took two weeks for the government to intervene. During this time, students just idled away as their reading passion waned. When the examination finally took place, predictably, Billy and Obaedo did very well when the results were released. They both went home for the short break before the resumption of the second semester. On resumption, they saw new lecturers appointed into their respective departments. The local association of lecturers had made much heat about the recruitment process. Alleging that a lot of ethnicity and corrupt practices trailed the whole exercise, they demanded that it should be cancelled. Not only were the appointments not advertised, the new appointees had not been formally interviewed. The appointees were given temporary appointments letters which would be regularized later. But the university authorities stood their ground that the exercise was transparent even though the appointments were from the influence of very influential people in society.

The second semester began with a lot of politicking for the students' union elections. The whole campus was electrified by the political mood. Every available space was covered in colourful handbills especially those of Richard Abu who was rumoured to be backed by the state governor. The contestants would go from class to class promising to do things that were clearly beyond their authority. On Election Day, the peaceful conduct of the elections was marred as the university authorities suddenly cancelled the entire process and rescheduled the elections. Anger and protests filled the campus until a detachment of anti-riot police men were sent in and the school was closed for over a month. There were witnesses who said the policemen raped many female students in the process. One known casualty was Ejiro Okiemute, a 300 Levels student of Biochemistry, who was hit by a stray bullet. As he laid down bleeding and losing strength, he spoke to those around in the pidgin language, 'Una dey look me? Bros na go I dey so o." Before a car could be got to rush him to the Health Centre, the young man died. An elderly security guard who had tried to get a car to rush Ejiro to the hospital, stood sober, watching the lifeless body.

"This life is nothing," he finally muttered.

On resumption, every student had to produce a letter attesting to be of good behavior and failing which they could be expelled. The elections were finally held and the students' favourite, Cosmos Ortega, a young medical student with fiery oratory won. His supporters took the whole day celebrating around campus.

The university football cup tournament was a yearly event during the second semester and was sponsored by the Bank of the Niger. There were cash prizes for the winning team, the runners-up, the highest goal scorer and the most valuable player. Billy had decided to join the practice sessions for his faculty team. Although he put in much effort, he was not chosen in the first eleven players. He had to be content with being in the reserves. The talk of campus was the Engineering football team nicknamed 'Engine'. They had dominated the football tournament for years and few people believed any other team on campus could beat them within the 90 minutes regulation time. Billy's Law team through good footballing skills and sheer luck eventually qualified for the finals to face the indomitable Engine. Billy had not been used throughout the knock out stages but kept his cool. The football final was a very colourful event attended by the vice chancellor and other senior university management staff. The MD of Bank of the Niger came from headquarters with a lot of their bank executives and staff. Students and members of the public thronged the University Sports Complex. The special guest of honour was the state commissioner of sports, the energetic Prince Dele Ikhide. The Law team played according to the instructions of their coach, Dr. Emmanuel Madu, their Criminal Law lecturer who kept barking out instructions to them and gesticulating from the touchline. The team was able to neutralize constant barrage of attacks from the Engineering team. For a team that had scored twenty goals on their way to the finals, many could not believe that as the match entered its last ten minutes, the score was still goalless. Then a defensive mistake was capitalized on by Festus Ikhimi, the tournament top scorer. He beautifully rounded up the Law goal keeper and scored what appeared the winning goal. The crowd erupted in cheers. The drumming and singing by the Engineering supporters increased. It was then that Dr. Madu decided to effect a change. Perhaps it was his master stroke or just sheer instinct but he brought in Billy who though had impressed during practice had never kicked a ball throughout the competition. It was barely minutes to the end of the match and Billy just took a shot to the goal of the opponent and the goal keeper who had not been tested throughout the match swung and tipped the ball over the bar. The crowd cheered. From the resultant corner kick, Billy who stayed outside the '18' yard box and unmarked, had the ball headed out to his direction. He didn't even contemplate but struck at it with all his strength and it flew past the goal keeper into the top corner of the net. The crowd went berserk. Billy's colleagues all jumped upon him. Obaedo was weeping. The referee gave 5 minutes of injury time in which the Engineering team marshaled all their skills and strength to win the match in regulation time. But the Law team held on. It then went straight to penalties. Billy was chosen to kick his team's last penalty. After the first four kicks by each team, the score was 4-4. Then Festus Ikhimi stepped forward to kick his team's fifth penalty. Whether it was nervousness or bad luck but his kick went over the bar. There was a loud gasp from the crowd. Ikhimi broke down, fell on his knees. The Engineering team supporters went quiet. The eyes of everyone was on Billy, this young first year student who was not even a regular member of his team, the first eleven. The Engineering goalkeeper tried to play eye games with him but he kept his eyes on the ball. As the referee gave him the signal to shoot, he aimed his body to the left and the goal keeper leapt there but Billy calmly swayed his shot to the opposite direction into the goal. The pitch was invaded by the exultant crowd. Billy was carried shoulder high by his team mates. Obaedo broke down crying uncontrollably in the stands. All around in the VIP box, the special dignitaries were talking excitedly. There were happy faces everywhere. The MD of Bank of the Niger, Olomide Olorunibe presented the Cup to the Law team captain and the cash prize of a N100, 000 naira. To the delight of all, Billy was named the most valuable player of the tournament and was presented a Bank plaque with a cash prize of N50, 000 naira. He was all smiles as he collected. The state television station interviewed him for the news slot and he expressed himself confidently. Obaedo would buy him a gift of a little perfume and a card the next day with a heading, 'Congratulations!', printed in gold. Inside she wrote a little message: 'You inspired us all. Oba.'

Part of the activities of the English Week was a Shakespearean Night organized by Obaedo's English department. The student best able to recite and put life into a long enough quotation from any of Shakespeare's work was to receive a prize. In all ten students had enrolled to take part, including Obaedo. She won the prize for dramatizing so well Jaques words to Duke Senior in As You Like It:

All the world's a stage,

And all the men and women merely players;

They have their exits and their entrances,

And one man in his time plays many parts,

His acts being seven ages. At first, the infant,

Mewling and puking in the nurse's arms.

Then the whining schoolboy, with his satchel

And shining morning face, creeping like snail

Unwillingly to school. And then the lover,

Sighing like furnace, with a woeful ballad

Made to his mistress' eyebrow. Then a soldier,

Full of strange oaths and bearded like the pard,

Jealous in honor, sudden and quick in quarrel,

Seeking the bubble reputation

Even in the cannon's mouth. And then the justice,

In fair round belly with good capon lined,

With eyes severe and beard of formal cut,

Full of wise saws and modern instances;

And so he plays his part. The sixth age shifts

Into the lean and slippered pantaloon,

With spectacles on nose and pouch on side;

His youthful hose, well saved, a world too wide

For his shrunk shank, and his big manly voice,

Turning again toward childish treble, pipes

And whistles in his sound. Last scene of all,

That ends this strange eventful history,

Is second childishness and mere oblivion,

Sans teeth, sans eyes, sans taste, sans everything.

By the time they were finishing their second semester examinations of their first year in the university, Obaedo had put off so many advances from boys. She had refused further invitations to go out with Woke and the young lecturer during the first semester. Happily, nothing had gone wrong. But this time, there was a new kind of pressure. The pressure on her was from a different quarter and it was heavier.

Chapter 7
Showing Care.

The time for national and state elections came around again and the political terrain entered into a high gear. Chief Famous Edeniyere who had been dropping hints all along that he will go for his party's ticket to run as governor of the state announced his intention on February 22, 2002. That same day as Billy and Obaedo read together, they both talked with excitement about Chief Edeniyere becoming governor. Billy also told Obaedo that Anti-communist UNITA guerilla leader Jonas Savimbi was killed in a clash against government troops led by socialist Angolan President José Eduardo dos Santos in Moxico Province, Angola. The death would gradually end the fighting that had lasted since 1975. The civil war ended on April 4.

Chief Edeniyere had constantly developed a political base across all local government councils of the state and with his huge financial chest and renowned patronage, many knew he will become his party's flag bearer even though the out-going ailing governor preferred his own son-in-law who was his special adviser on health, to succeed him. The party primaries was keenly contested and much money changed hands. Eventually, Chief Edeniyere was pronounced the winner. It was 10 October, 2002 and the International Court of Justice (ICJ) ruled against Nigeria in favour of Cameroon over the disputed oil – rich Bakassi peninsula territory. Chief Edeniyere would now bring in his wealth of politicking and resources as he transversed all areas of the state in his campaign to become the next governor. His political rallies were colourful, food and drinks were freely shared. It was rumoured that on coming to any town, he had a special gift for the traditional ruler of the place, which was said to be cash in millions of naira. The local town youth and women bodies were not left out from the largesse.

"When I become your governor on May 29th, by the special grace of God, I will rule this great state through wards and village assemblies", he had said during his final campaign rally in Benin.

"Of course the state House of Assembly will continue their work, that is if they want to work at all."

The crowd released an outburst of prolonged laughter.

"My approach will be to govern from the grassroots up. Every ward and village will have their own special assemblies where people will meet and decide on the needs for the area. A certain percentage of taxes collected from each ward must be plowed back into that ward for development."

The crowd shouted and cheered.

"From these wards, we will set up ward revenue committees to collect government taxes from businesses in those wards. Apart from giving employment which salary will be paid from the percentage of collected taxes from that ward, it will also bring in some civility. These tax officers will be collecting taxes from those they already know who stay in the same ward with them. I hardly imagine they will need inflict violent on their neighbours just to collect taxes. Anyway, the percentage of collected tax that will go to their ward should make businesses in those wards to pay up their taxes. No need to act as if we are in the jungle. I do not need touts to collect taxes. Touts, roughnecks should be in the farms.

"You see, my father taught me many things but he did not teach me how to steal. I am not now about to start doing things which my father never taught me. I am not going into Government House to steal public funds. It is badly brought up children who grow up into irresponsible adults who do that. The state's revenue will be for the state development."

They all applauded in excitement.

"My salary will be enough for me, my wife and my twin daughters. I don't live a wayward life so I don't have girlfriends to share money to who will in turn share HIV to me. I respect my wife too much to have her be a First Lady who shares her husband with harlots."

There was prolonged laughter.

"One reason why people in government behave so abnormally, behaviours that you just cannot understand, outright stealing, is that many of them apart from the dark spirits that they worship which have turned their hearts, many have sexually transmitted diseases affecting their brain. How can a man with gonorrhea, syphilis, think clearly? These things affect the human brain."

There was another outburst of prolonged laughter.

"I have my scientific findings on this. Patronizing harlots have done much havoc on our nation, our leaders, so many of their brains are infected.

"Each ward will have its own security outfit, funded by every house paying a token fee to the state security trust fund. With this fund, we will equip the local hunters and incorporate local jaguda boys into our security outfit."

The crowd roared his nick name.

An Igbo man in the crowd shouted, *"Onwa!"*

"Odiegwu", his friend added.

"I am today sounding a note of warning to all criminals to start relocating from this state. Every person in every ward in the state will be registered along with your place of occupation or business. Landlords will compile their list of tenants and submit and will vouch for their tenants as responsible persons. Property owners will compile the list of all in their homes. Nobody will hide. Our security team will have vehicles for all the wards equipped with communication gadgets to rally with other security agencies. They will patrol their areas day and night and with their modern sophisticated hunting weapons, they will hunt down animals. Or will the federal government not allow us to hunt again"?

The place erupted knowing the complexity of bearing arms which the federal Police force jealously guards against non-formal security bodies possessing. But nothing stops traditional hunters who have used guns before the nation was created by the imperialist British.

"If Herdsmen can carry arms to protect their livestock which is not provided for in the constitution and are not harassed, we will arm our own special hunters to hunt down wild animals in our midst who are a threat to our existence as a people. I am not saying I am the messiah but I will transform this state and you all will be living witnesses."

Kris Okotie's song, his theme song for his campaign,

"I love, I love, I love you, Am always thinking about you",

started blaring out from the speakers. As Chief Edeniyere swayed back and forth, the crowd erupted in cheers and started dancing in different directions.

When the elections finally came, Chief Edeniyere trounced his rivals by a very wide margin and was sworn in as the new governor of the state on May 29, 2003. In his inaugural speech, he didn't fail to wow the crowd.

"Nigeria had a world status as a leading oil and gas producer. In the 1980s, we had four functional refineries, processing refined commercial crude oil for domestic consumption and export. Now, those refineries have been run aground despite the billions of dollars that have gone into the building and the refurbishing of these refineries. Nigeria has also laboured to establishing steel complexes. Iron ore deposit in Itakpe, Ajabanoko and Oshokoshoko all in the region around Kabba-Okene-Lokoja-Koton Karfe axis, led to the establishment of the Ajaokuta Steel Company. Right now, we are still yet to own a thriving steel plant. A steel plant will make Nigeria a major producer of industrial machinery, auto-electrical spare-parts, shipbuilding, railways and carriages.

What about our paper industries, Nigeria Paper Mill Limited, in Jebba, Kwara; the Nigeria Newsprint Manufacturing Company Limited, in Oku-Iboku, Akwa-Ibom; and the Nigeria National Paper Manufacturing Limited, in Ogun state. Bad management, corruption, have run them aground. What of the Nigeria Railway Corporation, the Nigerian Telecommunications Limited (NITEL), Nigeria Airways. Now many developed nations that I have been to have corrupt leaders too but they have managed to still prosper but ours is typical black witchcraftcy: destroy and kill. My good German friend, Professor Horst Keppler, is around to celebrate with me. Whenever I visit Germany, I stay in his mansion. He will be one of my unofficial advisers. He once told me something about our own country that shook me. He said, "Legitimate and illegitimate have no meaning in Nigeria. Because everything is corrupt, therefore nothing is corrupt."

What a statement. I was startled that an outsider knows us so well. I am not the Nigeria Messiah. The only Messiah is Jesus Christ. But I will try to make an impact in our state. You will see it from today. Executive powers given to any man is a very big thing, it can be used rightly or to destroy and kill. I am not a witch."

He then abolished the Saturday restriction of movement for environmental sanitation, saying it was anti-business.
"I don't need to restrict you to your homes like you are

children in a dormitory so as to tidy up your surroundings. You should do that daily. Our health officers will go round to bring out all those who want to live in filth. You will be fined.

Our market women have for too long suffered under the groan of undue and oppressive levies. These our mothers are heroes, striving to make ends meet and to make food available to us all. Why tax them? Tax your mother so you can spend the money on Ashewo? No wonder there are many who believe that we have cursed leaders. Henceforth, all levies on market women in this state are abolished. What I loose from their taxes I will get elsewhere."

There was spontaneous shouting from the crowd.

"I will also see to it that a special transport scheme is arranged for these women who wake up early to go to village markets to buy foodstuff for sale. Most times they return in very rickety and dangerous vehicles, risking their lives. We will ensure the transfer of such goods to urban areas is better handled. I know how unscrupulous police officers have targeted these women in the past, collecting filthy money from the drivers which are further passed on to us all in increase of food prices. By the time I set up this new transport scheme for these women, woe betide that police officer on the road that will try to stop my vehicles…"

The whole place erupted with shout of 'lion.'

"And our city commercial drivers, much have been made of their recklessness and rudeness. I won't be a real governor if I don't push to ensure civility prevails in our society. We shall set up a mobile court for our commercial drivers. All those found driving recklessly, driving with excessive speed and generally being a nuisance amongst people, they don't belong to our cities. We will have psychiatric test for such drivers and they will sentenced to work in our rural farms which we are going to set up. By the time they farm for three years, their senses will return."

He was to speak for four hours but there was never a boring moment.

Everyone in the massive crowd, who came to witness his swearing-in, each had a good portion of *jollof rice*, meat and a soft drink given them on their way home.

....

....

Obaedo had continued to attend Bishop Azuka's Last Days Apostolic Perfection Church. She was now in the choir and still enjoyed the services especially the atmosphere. She had started getting undue attention and favours from Nduka, the Bishop's son, which earned her some side talks from other sisters in the choir. When some new songs were to be tried, Nduka would always want Obaedo to give it a try before others. And when she sang her first special song in church, Nduka made sure the musicians gave her the best melody. Something had happened after one song rehearsal on a Saturday. Nduka who was still a bachelor had offered to drop her off at her brother's place but told her to cross over the street to a junction and wait. He didn't want anyone knowing he was giving her a lift in his car. Bashfully, she agreed. Just as he showed up to pick her up, Ifeyinwa rode up and saw them. She looked at Obaedo scornfully and drove away. Instead of just taking her home, Nduka drove to the Government Reserved Area [GRA] of the city to a popular Chinese restaurant. He took her to a secluded section away from the main hall. He ordered a lavish meal. Obaedo had never been treated to such lately. Although she enjoyed it she was quite nervous.

By the time Nduka dropped her at her brother's, it was already late. He put a crisp collection of money notes into her hands saying 'for your handouts'. Johnson was a bit surprised to see her returning late and being dropped by Nduka. He said nothing to her. Nduka would continue pestering Obaedo for outings and started visiting her in school. She respected him as the Bishop's son but she knew Billy was a far better guy. When she was out dinning with him that Saturday, she told him casually about Billy. His reaction was expressionless especially when she had said he was like a confidant to her.

True to it, Obaedo had continued to confide in Billy all the affection and attention she was receiving from Nduka. She would also tell him of the many sermons of the Bishop who would more and more with each service, paint a picture of his special place for Christians of the day. To this, Billy would say, 'Is he not just blowing his own trumpet?'

Obaedo enjoyed the services especially the delivery method of the Bishop and his charisma. He could be real moving. The musical ministry was so organized and effective as well as the choir. Nduka always pushed them to give their best. One Sunday, the Bishop had announced that a special youth service would be held on Friday evening and that Nduka would preach the sermon. Obaedo who had never heard him preach the Word, looked forward to what he would say. He didn't seem like someone called to preach. He spoke about his father's ministry being a sort of God's spokesman like the apostle Peter was on the Day of Pentecost, who people must listen to in order to be saved. He had before his sermon, sang a special song, titled, 'There Is None Like You.' He would later tell her one night in Lagos that he was singing about her that night.

After the service and in the Car Park, Nduka who was greeting other members, saw Obaedo and moved to her and asked her how he did. She noticed that another Sister, Carrie, somewhat reacted negatively on hearing this question. Obaedo just said it was fine. On getting home, she asked her brother about Carrie.

"She has been close to Nduka through the years especially in the choir. People somehow believe that Nduka would marry her because he had been very caring towards her. But Nduka generally shows such care to other sisters anyway."

Obaedo had felt a bit shocked at this display of affection towards many sisters. She began to think of the reactions of sisters in the choir when Nduka seemed to push her up. Were they just expressing their female tendencies because he was also close to them?

One Sunday, the Bishop lambasted Sister Glory who was not in the service. Infact she never returned. From the sermon, the picture was painted of a sister pushing herself on his son for marriage through blackmail. The Bishop thundering out like fire was coming from his eyes declared that his son was fully into Christ work and no wayward girl should sneak into his church and bring a harlot spirit into his church. Many members were echoing loud 'Amens!' as he spoke.

Chapter 8
Politeness.

As their years in school went on, Obaedo and Billy kept up in their education with good success. Billy would continue being his calm studious self while Obaedo who became more pretty with each year, was now very attractive. She was still as bright as ever with her heart-stopping tenderness. Many on campus still regarded them as boyfriend and girlfriend because of their closeness. Obaedo had continued to resist advances from male students and some lecturers. Even in the Bishop's church, she also had to fend off some undue attention from some brothers even as the Bishop's son continued his undue affection. She had once asked a course mate if boys pestered her.

"Except you are not a girl then. Most every lady experiences these things. Sadly many of us give in most of the time. I know of many of our course mates who would confide in another girl the sordid details of her outing with a boy. And then that other girl would also tell another girl and the news will eventually spread. Truth is many female undergraduates are really turned into amateur prostitutes by boys. They would continually pester you until they wear you out. It takes a real strong conviction to remain a virgin through the university."

....
....

One of his first acts on becoming state governor, apart from sending his list of nominees for commissioners to the House of Assembly for screening, was for Chief Edeniyere to announce the privatization of the state transport company. There was grumbling when it was announced that the governor's own private transport company won the bid. The state transport company, JAGUAR, had been badly run for years. Many months' salary and pension were owed workers.

"Look, I am no more chairman of SAVANNAH TRAILS you hear. They bided and won a transparent transaction. But who among you have not enjoyed the services of SAVANNAH TRAILS through the years. Eh? Even foreigners have. Their efficiency is second to none. Or do you rather the state sell its assets to lazy incompetent politicians? Our people returning from overseas, when they land at Lagos airport, they immediately book SAVANNAH TRAILS for their journey to Benin. Why? Because they know it is almost certain they will arrive body and soul together in Benin. They know the bus they are entering is mechanically sound and won't be driven by an Indian-hemp ravaged-brain driver, who rely on fetish for safe trips." Chief Edeniyere had replied to probing questions from the press.

True to SAVANNAH TRAILS legacy of efficiency, they injected new blood into the JAGUAR. They did things with the speed of a Jaguar. All backlog of salaries and pensions were cleared. All staff were made to reapply. Those who were deemed not sharp enough and business-inclined were retired with huge benefits. This went down well with the people of the state. Massive new employment was carried out after a very strenuous recruitment process meant to target business minded individuals and cool-headed drivers. Prospective drivers went through an excruciating interview process and tests for their provocation and humility level. Only the best were given employment. Brand new buses were imported and introduced in addition to creating new inter cities and states routes. Air-conditioned Taxi cabs were introduced in Benin City with a special section solely for doing school run for parents. Before long, many had come to accept the wisdom of having SAVANNAH TRAILS take over the state moribund transport company. The governor soon after inaugurated a committee to help the JAGUAR go into airline business. The state was agog on the day of the announcement. He also used that occasion to announce the signing of a memorandum of understanding with a South African firm that will turn the Ikpoba riverside area into a viable commercial and recreational mini city to include shopping malls, boat sailing, hotels and any other project that will make that area a tourist and commercial attraction. The audience burst out into frenzy, shouting 'lion'

....

....

Time flew by and the semesters came and gone, dry season followed the rains. With each succeeding year, Billy and Obaedo surmounted the challenges of obtaining a formal university education and excelled in their exams. Just as they prepared to write their first semester examinations in their final year, another wave of students' riot broke out and the university had to be closed down for a month. As part of Students Week, the students Exco had invited fiery Ijaw Marxist, Tamuno to speak. He has a history of throwing students into wild frenzy whenever he spoke. Always dressed casually with a slippers and heavy beards, he speaks slowly at first, watching his every word, then raising up his voice, until the crowd is gripped. He had been arrested several times by various military governments.

The 500LT venue of the lecture was overfilled as many came to catch a glimpse of this renown professor of Political Science. The vice chancellor and the university management had stayed away even though they were invited.

"England with its imperialist arrogance colonised Nigeria and ran it for their selfish needs."

The students clapped.

"They added salt to our injury in 1914 by amalgamating the poor North with the rich South. They blatantly did this and held us their colonized slaves captive without consultation or agreement for 46 years. Feeling the heat, they gave us a Greek gift of independence in 1960 and our leaders fell for it even when it was obvious that they had imposed a fraudulent census data on us that enabled them to rig the elections and hand over power to the North. Now, they did not give power to true northerners like Aminu Kano, Sir Kashim Ibrahim, incorruptible men, who had the peoples' welfare at heart. No, it was to the same elite which had oppressed the common northerners before the British came and who they also worked with before Independence. This elite that are so haughty and uplifted from the commoners, are experts in the tools of governmental coercion, detentions, imprisonment, oppression and corrupt practices. These are the ones that the British gave political and military powers to. They got both political and military powers but they were un-informed and visionless. They didn't know what to do with it apart from scheming to have everybody kneeling down before them and to marrying many wives. Their incompetence came to the fore and things began to fall on their head. The prime minister was reporting to the Northern Premier in violent desecration of the constitution so as to entrench Northern elite interest and hegemony not northern people interest. Their own private interest.

Coups had taken place in Africa before that of Nigeria in 1966, but the same British instigated the Northern elite to declare the coup of January 1966 an Igbo coup. The same British watched with glee, doing nothing as instigated common Northerners butchered Igbos in their thousands. The ferocity and savagery of this pogrom is not yet matched, even in modern terrorist territories and activities. After the Aburi Accord to temper things down, the same Britain educated the Northern elite that the agreement will prevent them from their continued exploitation of the rest of the country as the new overlords. Almost two million lives were lost in the ensuing war. The use of hunger and starvation as instruments of war, even if against women and children was introduced with the British still watching and applauding."

There were cries of revulsion from the crowd.

"The victorious, Northern elite army became the full Nigeria army of fortune. With British support, this army re-colonised Nigeria and established a corrupt political hegemony with a rudderless leadership class that rotates between the Northern military and their civilian political wing. They have continually drunk the wealth from the oil in our creeks and swamps leaving our people even without clean water. Fishing has been ruined, our environment polluted. No thought has been spared ordinary Nigerians, nothing for its youths and nothing for their future. Even the free feeding normally enjoyed by university undergraduates was stopped and tuition increased. And according to Franz Fanon, Each generation must discover its mission, fulfill it or betray it. If we don't…"

At this time, a known students' activist, Muyiwa Olawale jumped on the high table and started screaming wildly, clearly instigated by the speech.

"Down with the tyrants!!!"

Like a possessed man, the gathered students all stood up like one man, joining him. They then broke out from the hall and made their way to the vice chancellor's office. Professor Uyi Ugiagbe had a premonition that there might be trouble. As he heard the noise of students approaching, he was seen fleeing, leaving behind his official vehicle. The students thrashed the vice chancellor's office then made their way to the Ugbowo-Lagos highway and blocked it, smashing vehicles' windscreen and harassing their occupants. The army Brigade commander who was caught up in the ensuing long traffic, phoned the state commissioner of police but could not reach him as his aide had said he had given strict instruction to be left alone undisturbed. By the time the brigade commander got through to the governor, the commissioner of police, Edun Omotola, had come out of his office with a young university girl and he then phoned the governor. He then marshaled his men to go quash the riot. The huge destruction occasioned by the students' riot cost the vice chancellor and the commissioner of police their jobs.

Finally after five plus years, due to disruptions by mindless industrial actions by academic and administrative staff at different times, and students' wildcat riots, Obaedo and Billy graduated from the University of Benin, with distinctions. They both made a Second Class Upper division. They both wrote their undergraduate academic thesis which had given them much stress. They put in much effort and then successfully defended their project work before Christmas, 2004. On December 26, 2004, Boxing Day, Billy visited Obaedo in her father's house to spend the day together. They ate much and talked of their many experiences through their undergraduate years. On that day, they watched on CNN as one of the worst natural disasters in recorded history hit Southeast Asia. The strongest earthquake in 40 years, measuring 9.3 on the Richter scale, hit the entire Indian Ocean region, generating an enormous tsunami that crashed into the coastal areas of a number of nations including Thailand, India, Sri Lanka, the Maldives, Malaysia, Myanmar, Bangladesh, and Indonesia. The official death toll in the affected countries was put at 186,983. It was much more than that.

Billy and Obaedo also spent New Year Day together in her father's house. Then he went to Lagos to attend the Nigerian Law School on February Feb 15, 2005, the day, YouTube, the popular video sharing website, was founded. Obaedo was later posted to Abuja for her mandatory National Youth Service. She served as a teacher in an outskirt government school in Gwagwalada. She continually kept in touch with Billy, mostly at night. Billy settled down easily in his hostel at the Nigerian Law School enjoying the scenic Lagos lagoon view from his window. He looked forward to attending his classes very much and found the courses very interesting.

Somewhere half way through her service year, Obaedo was shocked one day as the principal sent for her as she had a visitor. It was Nduka. She was shocked but controlled herself. He had somehow found out about her place of primary posting. Not knowing what to do, she led him out of the Principal's office. He looked so excited telling her he just came to see how she was doing.

"You took all this pain just to come see me? I am okay."

Nduka was staying in a hotel in Abuja and wanted her to come visit him after work. She tried to fend him off but he persisted. She would later go but remained in the Reception Hall. It was October 22nd, 2005 and Abuja had been gripped by the news of the death of Stella Obasanjo, wife of Nigeria's president who died in Malaga Spain shortly after cosmetic surgery. Nduka took her to the restaurant where he spent a lot on the food. It was a five star hotel. When he asked her if she wouldn't come to see his room upstairs, she declined politely saying she should be on her way back to the Corpers' Lodge on the outskirts of town. To her surprise, Nduka while folding something into her hand, kissed her on her lips. She was shocked and put off but some white folks in the restaurant didn't seem to mind. Nduka noticing her distress apologized saying that he really came to be with her for two days. She stood up angrily to go. He followed her and beckoned on a hotel taxi to take her. He paid off the driver. Back in her room at the Corpers' Lodge, thoughts raced through her mind on Nduka's behaviour at the restaurant and for the past five years. She knew, as a woman, what Nduka was driving at but she just could not muster up the boldness to rudely tell him off. But did she really like him? Of course not, she shouted to herself. But after all she was still in his father's church and could not afford to be rude to him, she thought. But why does he not know better, she asked to nobody in particular. Where is the godly character and behavior that ought to accompany his profession as a youth preacher, a Bishop's son and a church official? Is he even Christianly saved? Despite the many things he had done for her, going out of his way to please her, she didn't really see him as an ideal young man or even a life partner. He was the alpha type of male, a go-getter who was too free with ladies and will turn out to be most irresponsible. Once in the female rest room in church after a service, she had overheard two sisters run Nduka down for his indecent acts with sisters and other non-believing girls. But since the Bishop was always lambasting gossiping against his family, she just didn't give heed to the sisters' side talk. One of them, Irenegbe, seemed more bitter as she made an ugly remark of Nduka's inner goal being to see the nakedness of every young lady in church. The other, Oge, concurred. It was on the very day that the Bishop had severely rebuked and derided with very strong words Brother Joe and Sister Kemi, who had fallen into fornication. Brother Joe had begun to be attracted to Sister Kemi since she first came to join the assembly. He would stay very close to Kemi after services, making sneak attempts to chat her up. He would also go visit her at her workplace at the University of Benin Teaching Hospital, where she was a nurse. He started nursing ideas of getting married to her. Kemi grew to like his person and with his gifts and attention, she got carried away. She had cooked him a delicious meal on his birthday and went to his house early on a Saturday to surprise him. Brother Joe was speechless. He owned a Printing House and was quite comfortable. He was overwhelmed with the presence of Kemi and the treat for his birthday. He decided not to go to work that day but called his boys to handle things. With all the excitement of being together, before long, they had gotten intimate and fallen into sin. Sister Olumi had seen Kemi leaving Brother Joe's house late in the evening and she went straight to report to Ifeyinwa, the Bishop's daughter. On interrogation, she confessed and was roundly scolded and humiliated by Ifeyinwa. The next Sunday service was dedicated to both of them.

While serving in Abuja, Obaedo was still a centre of men's attraction especially at events where corpers attended. Once at a government forum for corpers, Femi Badejo, the local branch manager of Unity Bank that was sponsoring the event tried to keep her in a long conversation even though they had never met before. Back at the Corpers' Lodge, some female corpers teased her about missing her chance with the manager. When she replied she was not interested, they mocked her, "But you were smiling ear to ear, talking with him."

"I had to be polite you know."

"Polite? How many girls have we seen politeness made to fall inside a pot of soup", countered Esosa, a dark Bini girl. "Instead of calling off their antics, you smile sheepishly until they make you another statistics and move on. Men?" she hissed.

Obaedo would continue to face more attention until she passed out from service especially from fellow male youth corpers. Though she kept being polite, things never turned ugly.

As part of her Community Development Service, Obaedo had an artist design two signposts which were erected on the Abuja-Lokoja Highway. They read, 'Drive To Arrive Safely. Your Loved Ones Are Waiting For You.' and 'Speed Thrills Before It Kills. Please Control Yourself.' They are still there today.

Chapter 9
Politeness Still.

Obaedo returned back to Benin City after her passing-out from her National Youth service in Abuja. Through her father's influence she got an assistant lecturer position at the department of English, Literature and Classics, University of Benin. She started work on May 16, 2006, the day the National Assembly of Nigeria voted against a constitutional amendment to remove term limits. President Obasanjo was effectively prevented from contesting a third term in office. Obaedo immediately started her Masters' degree programme. She quickly struck a friendship with a vivacious young Bini female lecturer in her department, Ms. Ameze, who with her lively wit and sassy ways kept her up lively in conversations and good company. Ameze was a tall dark-complexioned girl in her late 20's, the type of girl who would only tell you 'Good morning' because she meant it. She is very attractive looking, bright and has a natural tendency to speak profane but sometimes in a nice sort of way. She has a brilliant mind with a courageous spirit and with wisdom beyond her years, it's almost impossible not to like her.

"Have you heard the weather forecast for tonight: it's going to be dark," she once said on entering Obaedo's office one morning.

Once in a departmental academic meeting, Professor Julius Osahon, the Head of Department, midway into the meeting realizing that they hadn't made plans for refreshment, started asking what each lecturer would like so that it can be ordered for.

"A Range Rover fully air-conditioned would be okay for me Prof.", Ameze had said.

Everyone turned to look at her.

The HOD shook his head.

"Coke", "Fanta", "Chilled malt", "Eggroll and Pepsi", "Roasted chicken", the others kept on with their needs.

Obaedo had been given an apartment at the senior staff quarters to her great delight. This gave her the opportunity to beautify the house to her taste. The kitchen, living room and her bedroom were exquisitely furnished, paid for by her father. She had used much of her initial pay to stock a mini library at home. Ameze's apartment was also close by and she would stroll to Obaedo's house most evenings and they would cook and eat, discussing most everything. With time, Obaedo would come to know Ameze as one of those few women who have admiration and respect for other women that have attributes that they themselves do not possess. Obaedo liked her person. She even encouraged Ameze to follow her to their church one Sunday. Though not a very churchy girl, she agreed to accompany Obaedo. After the service as they were about driving out, Nduka had come to greet Obaedo and inquired about her friend.

"Hi, hope you will come back?"

Ameze didn't reply, wearing an emotionless straight face. Driving out, Obaedo asked her why she was that cold to Nduka.

"There is just something about him that I don't like. He is a very subtle spirit."

"Ameze! But you only just met him."

"I saw him mouthing and bouncing in the pulpit like a basketball. I am a good judge of character Obaedo. Moreover I have seen his kind before. They are all about…"

Obaedo cut in laughing, "Girl! But anyway, how was the service?"

"I won't come again. Never."

"You mean you didn't get anything from the sermon?"

"I have two books at my bedside, the King James Bible of our Lord and the complete Works of William Shakespeare. They have proven to be wellspring of undiluted truth and inspiration to me. I am where I am today because I put no faith in obnoxious church megalomaniacs who relish the twin demonic pleasure of power and fame. They have populated the world today with their unbridled lust for ego gratification. If I wanted to hear a man boast shamelessly of who he thinks he is, I will slot in the film of David Koresh of Waco, Texas."

Obaedo was trying not to laugh.

"Jim Jones would have been very pleased taking notes here. I am however relieved that the excessive unrestrained zeal of the church members to idolise the person of their Bishop has not eaten into you to affect your character."

Obaedo glared at her playfully.

"Am serious. Look, this whole thing is expert manipulation. Just invite Dr. Ola to accompany you one day and you will hear a mouthful. You know he had his Masters in Psychology. This his kind all started out seemingly okay on the surface but then later become doomsday for their denuded followers. The mask of super-friendliness and hospitality shown to people only covers up real hideous things including total domination of people's lives. I mean TOTAL. This is a perfect setting to control people who are made to lose their reason to just follow a man unquestionably and in fear of damnation. I get his theme, 'If you leave me, you perish.' Damn him to hell!"

"Ame! But he was merely preaching from the Bible"

"Girl, be wary of those who preach from the Bible but do not preach the Bible. Even Satan quotes the Scriptures Obaedo. Was that portion removed from your Shakespeare's Merchant of Venice when you read it?"

Ameze proceeded to quote Shakespeare: *"The devil can cite Scripture for his purpose. An evil soul producing holy witness is like a villain with a smiling cheek, a goodly apple rotten at the heart. O, what a goodly outside falsehood hath!"*

" 'The truth of the Word for this day has come to me.' ", said Ameze mockingly mimicking Bishop Azuka. "Does he even know what the truth is? He can't handle the truth. Preachers? They are the greatest trick the devil ever pulled."

"My Prof! I just enjoy the services especially the atmosphere."

Ameze looked at Obaedo's face and then turned away to look out through the car side window, keeping a straight face.

They drove to Obaedo's favourite restaurant to collect her favourite snacks and then decided to go see the huge ongoing construction works at the Ikpoba riverside new mini city. True to his words, Governor Edeniyere had backed up the memorandum he signed with the South African company with state backed loans. It was truly touching for Obaedo because she grew up in her father's house which is close to the Ikpoba River and now so close to this new mini city. The entire area was now being transformed. The new state agency superintending the project, the Ikpoba River City Agency with a South African management team was creating a commercial avenue of well-paved broad roads on either side of the banks of the Ikpoba River. These avenues bothering the river bank on completion, will be comparable to world-famous shopping districts like Ramblas Street in Barcelona and Oxford Street in London. These waterside streets will become the nerve economic centre of the city. This dual-street avenue on either sides of the river bank, will have promenades and water fountains. Plots had already been allocated to private investors to build hotels, shopping malls, a theatre, events-halls for public reception, relaxation spots, stores and other activities of social and economic interests. Apart from the beauty it will give to the state capital, there are so many economic openings to be achieved from this endeavour. Many state indigenes in the Diaspora were lured to key in and invest. As usual, rumour went round that many of them including the South African company were business fronts for the governor.

"They are talking of fronts but action is happening there", the governor had retorted at one occasion. "Let those who have no fronts but back come and run the state aground." He hissed to the outburst of laughter from the audience.

"This new nerve Centre of entrepreneurship, relaxation and tourism will truly open up Benin City", Ameze said.
"Yes."

A young man also observing the site came near to them and tried to start a light conversation with Ameze.

"Aside from your face, what other jokes do you have?" Ameze asked him as she turned rudely away from him leaving him embarrassed.

"Did you have to treat him like that?", asked Obaedo quietly.

"I'd rather listen to paint dry. He is as intelligent as a lemon."

"But even a blind squirrel finds a nut every once in a while," said Obaedo laughing.

"My shoe is bigger than his car."

As they looked over the place, Obaedo thought to herself that the man spearheading all this was a family friend. She remembered the gift he had given her during her graduation from Secondary School and smiled to herself.

On getting home, they both prepared a Chicken stew while munching on the snacks.

"The perfume you wore today was a hit. I liked it. But did you need to have soaked your dress into the bottle," Ameze asked.
Obaedo eyed her.

Obaedo had introduced her brother Johnson to Ameze as they met in the church car park that morning. Now she tore into him.

'Your brother looked like a passport picture; he needs to find another job. If being a medical consultant doesn't make him happy then he needs to find something that will. He looked like a starved monk studying to be a hermit."

Obaedo looked at her and shook her head.

"What?", countered Ameze. "Obviously, also attending this church of yours, diving and falling all over the floor like a drunken sailor has not improved him."

Obaedo was laughing.

"No matter how he wants to dress it up to suit his conscience is immaterial. He has no joy. He looks quite pathetic. Quite sad for a professional. Whoever is seeing him look like that and yet holding him to that place, I will say they are an utter disgrace."

"Ame! Please bring me the curry."

"No need to bore himself to tears in a church. He should try watching paint dry. It will no doubt be a thrilling experience for him."

"You will one day win an Oscar for your mouth."

"You will win one for your stew."

After eating a late dinner, Obaedo walked Ameze down the road to her apartment. Here were two really pretty young women, bright and promising going down life's road full of youthful energy to becoming career intellectuals. Any stranger seeing them might have mistaken them for students as they had this air of ease and youthfulness. Decent and virgins, they were beautiful to look upon. The sky seemed the limit to what they will achieve. The cool evening wind played on their faces and long hair as the heat of the day had walked away from the earth. The sky was blue above and there were few cars running on the smooth roads. A lonely big mango tree by the side of the road looked down on them with calmness in her leaves as if it was admiring them.

"It is this type of evening that makes a walk interesting', said Ameze.

"You need to walk it with your admirer, the Bishop's son," Obaedo laughed.

Ameze hissed.

"When I want to marry, I'll marry for the conversation, it is the only thing that lasts. You know love is staying up all night with a sick child, or a healthy adult."

"What an exciting definition Ame"

"Does that one look like someone I can talk with? Just look at how you and your Tom Boy have come a long way, talking all the way."

Obaedo made a face of being mad at her. Obaedo had told her everything about Billy and their friendship from her secondary school days.

"Two of you can make music, you rhyme. You're together but not together yet."

"Thank you Ame."

"I saw both of you at your gate last week. You both have great chemistry. You are like a couple who can sit in the same room and send text messages to each other just for fun."

"O how I wish Billy was here to have eaten this delicious stew with us."

"Yea, to finish the whole pot", mocked Ameze.

"Yes, and I will make him pounded yam and egusi soup after that."

"I will empty your pepper can into the soup."

Billy had returned back to Benin after completing his Nigerian Law School programme and was now undergoing his mandatory National Youth Service in Benin City. He was posted to a leading Law firm in town. He invited Obaedo to come see him in his office once but she hadn't found the right time. As his service year was running out and being allowed to handle some cases in court, he invited her to come to court one day as he would be defending a bus driver arrested for over speeding. She went to the Magistrate's court and was happy seeing Billy doing what he enjoyed. The magistrate was a very tall man with a lean and hungry look. She figured that this type of magistrates can be real disciplinarians and heaven help all those who run foul of the law and are brought before them. After putting forth his case, the magistrate adjourned for some time to prepare his ruling on Billy's 'No case submission'. Billy took the opportunity to take Obaedo to the canteen. While they ate, they shared experiences in their jobs. Obaedo was again struck by Billy's gentlemanly ways, a far cry from Nduka. Billy had never pestered her but was so dear and loving, treating her like a real lady. Nduka was pushy, brash, always over stepping a woman's lines, yet religious. Her mind went back to how she and Billy had come far together right from their secondary school days. Now they were both graduates and doing fine. They got a surprise when they saw their old classmate Ero. He was so pleased to see them, calling Billy, master. He did not further his education after secondary school and ended up learning Water Bore Hole drilling. Now he was in court for taking money for a job not properly done. He had come to the canteen to buy his lawyer bottled water.

"You have put on much weight", Billy commented.

"Master, na life."

He then told Billy that he now had two children from his girlfriend.

"You are yet to marry her?"

"No, but she is staying with me. She has her own hair dressing salon. We manage together."

"But you should try go see her parents and do the correct thing. You need her parents' blessings to take their daughter."

"Yes, I will do that. I have already taken drinks to them."

"Okay, but do the complete thing."

Billy wished him well.

"Life can be very tough," Obaedo sighed.

"It is why I keep telling you, make your good judgments. Everyone have their challenges but you must be strong to confront them."

Billy knowing from Obaedo, her experiences with men, tried to encourage her about the men that kept coming at her.

"Many of them have bad motives but I trust your power of judgment and I know that you will make the best decisions."

"Thank you Bill."

"But try and avoid situations where you cannot resist nor think for yourself. Stay away from dangerous and negative atmosphere where due to pressure, women are made to do things they later regret. You have this earth, filled with men who are possessed with dark spirits fueling intense and unrestrained sexual craving, totally focused on a woman's looks and body. They are not in for having conversations, spending quality time or to get to meet her family and friends. A woman gets herself alone with such a man? Only one outcome I am afraid."

Obaedo listened as she remembered visiting Nduka in his hotel in Abuja. Billy had then been very sad when she had told him of what Nduka did to her. She imagined that things would have been worse had she not toughened up and refused to accompany him to his hotel room upstairs.

When they went back to court, the magistrate ruled in Billy's client favour, he struck out the case.

"As the Court pleases!!" roared out.

The jubilant bus driver and his friends thronged Billy outside the court room. He knelt down thanking him. Thinking Obaedo was his girlfriend, he knelt to her too, "Thank you madam, please help us thank Oga."

Billy told him to see them in chambers later in the evening to complete his payment.

"Yes Oga," he said and went on embracing his friends.

"Wow! You are the lawyer Richard Nixon could have hired to see him through Watergate," Obaedo complimented Billy.

"I am still in training my young Professor."

Since Obaedo came by public transport, Billy drove her back to her quarters at the University of Benin. He hesitated to enter saying he had to go back to the office. Obaedo wouldn't hear of it.

"Work, work, work. But where do you get your energy from? Ribena? Nigeria should enter you in the marathon at the next Olympics."

He briefly came into her living room. It was still as orderly and beautiful as the last time he came. Obaedo wanted to prepare something for him to eat but he refused. She had earlier told him she had a class to teach by 2pm and it was already past 1pm. He argued that she would miss her class if she went on to prepare the food. She hissed and said the students could wait forever. Billy laughed. She looked beautiful when she was angry. He succeeded in convincing her to go teach her students and he left.

Billy didn't hear from Obaedo for more than a week and her phone was off when he tried calling. Saturday morning, he decided to go see her at home. He knocked and it took some time for her to come open. He noticed she was real moody.

"What is it?", fear gripped him, his mind racing.

She sat down in her night gown on the long chair in the living room saying nothing for a while.

"Shall I prepare you something?" she finally asked.

"No, it is too early."

Her eyes seemed wet and he asked her again, this time softly, "Oba, what is it?"

Obaedo started weeping, sobbing. Billy was getting disturbed so he went to sit with her on the long chair. Her sobbing intensified as he sat close to her.

"Am so sorry, but whatever it is, let if off on me."

Obaedo tried to sober up, wiping her running nose with her wrapper. Billy gave her his handkerchief.

"He defiled me", Obaedo blurted out, crying again loudly.

"O dear, am so sorry."

Obaedo would not be consoled. Billy allowed her to cry.

When she stopped, he looked her and said, "Nduka?"

She nodded.

She then recounted how Nduka had wanted her to

accompany him to Lagos just to receive some church items that had arrived from overseas. He would be going with the morning flight and return the next morning he said. When she asked him if she alone was going with him, Nduka lied that a deacon was also coming along. It was when he handed her her ticket at the airport that she realized it was just the two of them. He then made some excuses that the deacon had some issues at work and won't be joining them. Asking if his father was aware she was coming with him, he replied that his father don't micro-manage his life.

"Woman, I am big enough to go anywhere and with anybody. I just need company."

Politeness, respect for him compelled her to agree to accompany him. During the flight, he explained that the clearing agent would bring the goods to their hotel for him to inspect and then return them to the airport to be placed in cargo for the next morning flight.

"Why then do you have to come down if he can send them down by flight?"

"But I have to see now what he is sending down. What if he just sends garbage?"

She wasn't convinced but just decided to enjoy the trip.

He booked two adjoining executive suites at the Sheraton hotel, Ikeja. He ordered room service and later they took a taxi to go shopping. They returned back to the hotel towards evening and Obaedo went to her room to get some rest. Nduka had bought her so many things she didn't ask for and seemed not to need. At 8pm, her intercom buzzed and woke her up. Nduka told her the agent was around with the goods. She went to his room to see modern electronic gadgets in well-arranged boxes. As the agent left and Obaedo wanted to return to her room, Nduka said, "Stay a little with me woman."

He said he wanted them to chat a little over a meal. He ordered room service and they started watching CNN. She didn't know when Nduka suddenly drew her to himself, kissed her on her mouth and started to fondle her hair.

"You shouldn't be doing this. You are a minister's son."

"O lecturer, lecturer, my lecturer. But I am a nigga also."

She got up to go back to her room but he went after her and hugged her from behind. Somehow her feminine gave in to his touching. She had never once been so held by any man. Then it happened so quickly, he moved her to his couch and he was all over her, making out. Whether it was over respect for his person or some other unexplainable reasons, she kept urging him to stop it and tried pushing him off her but didn't fight him off wildly like an angered lion would and bolt out as Nduka continued. He would later carry her despite her protest into the bedroom.

Nduka had already fallen asleep when she returned to her suite. She was ashamed and angry.

Thoughts raced through her mind from, "so this is what the sex is all about", to "another statistics."

She was so pained in having such a priced possession of hers so casually taken and by a boy who was certainly irresponsible. It now fully dawned on her that all the gossips made about him were true yet he was always stoutly defended by his father, a preacher of the Gospel. It dawned on her that no woman will be safe in this young man's company. This was not just corruption of youth but an unbridled satanic possession, a degenerate with a license to be devious. She also pondered how she would disclose this to Billy. It will surely break him. The kiss from Nduka in Abuja had hurt him. And then this. Knowing they had a morning flight to catch, she set her alarm to wake up by 5am. It was already past 2am. She barely slept.

Nduka knocked on her door saying their taxi was waiting to take them to the airport. He got a hotel staff to come carry their luggage down. Obaedo never uttered a word to him on their way to the airport and on the flight back to Benin. Thoughts just kept pouring into her mind. She was deeply offended by what this irresponsible young man had done. She was inwardly angry and his person offended her sense of refinement, her sense of being a Christian and of courteous behavior.

She took an airport taxi at Benin airport to her apartment, leaving behind all the things he had bought in Lagos for her.

Chapter 10
Best Friend.

She began sobbing again as Billy looked away. There was a moment of silence but she guessed she heard him muttering to himself,

"Something I cannot even see myself just taken so easily by…"

She was afraid on hearing this, not knowing what he would now do. His eyes were red, his mood was down.

Billy then spoke, looking into her eyes.

"Oba, you and I have come a long way together. I have known you to be a real decent woman. I have been proud of you through the years. I am a man, am certainly hurt and bitter but truth is you were caught up in a vicious trap of the enemy; you are a victim of a monstrous religious system. I know your trait; you will one day see the evil in this system. It is not founded on Christ. However, your courage, confiding in me makes me short of words. I thank you. I know you need some time to yourself to get over this. Try not to hurt yourself thinking. There is nothing you can really do now apart from reporting to the police which I do not think you will want to do because of the negative publicity. It is very painful. I am hurt, I cannot lie to you. I will try remain the Billy you ever knew."

Breaking from her sobbing as he spoke, she said, "Billy, I failed you. I failed my family. I have never known a man's love apart from my father and you. I respect you for who you are and am so sorry this happened."

She broke down again crying, "What have I done, oh what have I done to myself."

She looked broken and pitiable. He patted her on the back and left her apartment.

His drive back was pensive. The streets were largely free of cars inside the university as he drove out. Some elderly men that he sensed were professors were jogging along the Faculty road. Some students were playing a game of football in an open field and seemed caught up in the joy of youthful freedom. He noticed the lush green grass and imagined how young people see life so cool until it releases its dark side to them. His thoughts went back to Obaedo. He had always cherished her. She was a darling. His affection towards her seemed to be something away from what boys usually have towards girls. He hears their filthy conversation about girls. He had never really thought negative or romantic towards her but something in him always felt that she would make him a good companion later in life. And now, this. This is really saddening. Will things ever be the same between them? All because of one lunatic. He remembered when once he saw her father in court, how he had hugged him warmly and asked him, "How is Obaedo?"

"We don't see often sir. But I know she is fine."

He knew her father had some thoughts about both of them.

Along Wire road, he met a long line of cars held up by a police check point. He remembered the directive of the Inspector-general of Police banning all such police check points. When he got to the point of the officers, they tried chatting him up in a friendly way but he kept a straight face, saying nothing to them.

"Move on"

They were collecting money from commercial bus drivers and other road users that they could milk money from. It wasn't long ago that the governor's convoy ran into one such illegal check point and Governor Edeniyere had come out of his car and called the commissioner of police right from there. The commissioner of police replied that the men were on illegal duty and the governor had his security detail arrest the policemen who were all later dismissed from the force. Yet, others still went on with this illegality. The utter lawlessness further dampened his mood. Billy had some files to treat in the office that Saturday but he couldn't concentrate. His mind went back to Obaedo and her innocence that was taken away from her. He remembered how she looked sobbing. Pity overwhelmed him. He too broke down crying in his office.

"Lord, where were you when this happened?"

After he sobered up, he left his office and walked across the road to a football-viewing centre where vociferous young men were watching Chelsea Football Club play against Manchester United in the English Football League. He seemed to get a bit of relief. A young man came over to greet him. It was one of his former clients that he had pleaded bail for on his assault on his landlord. He smiled at him and kept watching the football match. By the time he got back home later in the evening, his mood had lifted a bit. He still had no appetite and had taken no food since morning. He went to check his email account and discovered Obaedo had sent him a mail': "My Best Friend"

'A woman's heart can race. A man she likes can do that. I have never had any other man do that through all the men I have dated. You alone hold that place. Since our secondary school days, to the university, to this moment, I have liked you. I told you of my outings with other boys and watched your reaction. You were not crude nor did you manifest any trace of jealousy. You seemed to trust my judgments. It encouraged me and gave me the confidence to open up to you easily. Billy, you always treat me like I'm amazing. Many men have told me that I am pretty but I don't feel it. You never once told me that, but I feel your silence on that more than

those who spoke it. You tell me I'm so brilliant even when I tell you I'm not. You spend all the time you can with me. You understand me. You have been amazing to know and to be with. Even if you decide not to tolerate me again for the rest of your life, I will cherish all the time you spent with me. But I am praying you forgive me and give me another chance. I like your genuine gentlemanliness. I like that you care for me and I need that more now in this strange world that we were born into. I didn't envisage that this would ever happen to me and I did my best as a woman to prevent it. Please forgive me. I need your company. I like your determination to excel in life. And especially, I like it that you're real. I like you Billy Onwundinjo.

Will remain yours,

Oba.'

Billy had wet eyes.

....
....

Governor Edeniyere had received the report of his transition committee headed by a young professor from the East, Professor Chuma Okolo. It had caused a storm when he had appointed a non-indigene of the state to head this important body. But he had dismissed their complaints telling them to wait and see. Having received their detailed report for transforming the state, he set about to implementing them step by step.

He sought the federal regulatory authority license and opened a new FM radio station, Eagle FM. It carried government news and announcements but was heavily commercial-based. The station harnessed the peoples' propensity for social lives; celebrations, weddings, birthdays, funerals, anniversaries and propagating businesses with a proper medium of commercial information dissemination. The radio station also featured continually the administration's programmes and top government officials frequently came on air to address and highlight issues. The governor had his own special talk show on Friday evenings, 7pm to 9pm aired on both state radio stations and the state television service. The talk show named The Governor, became very popular as Governor Edeniyere acted as the compere, talking on issues concerning his administration and taking calls from members of the public. He introduced brief commercial breaks of N500,000 naira per 30 seconds slot. Once a caller had wanted to know why he refused to buy the Local Christian Association a bus as they demanded.

"It is not for government to buy buses for churches. If they need one let them buy one for themselves from their own funds. Am sure their members pay enough into their churches. Moreover, it is this giving of cars, gifts, to churches and the clergy by government that makes them support evil in government. Because their mouth have been stuffed with largesse, they will see evil and they won't condemn it. Haven't we seen that before in this state? How can they boldly challenge me and hold me to account as men of God when they come seeking gifts from me? Yes I turned it down. Let them go and report me to God."

On another day, he touched raw nerve in speaking about corruption in government.

"People ask how I get the funds to run my programmes. The money has always been there. It is all a matter of priority. When people in government positions steal so much, they complain that there is no money. Look, if all the budgets in this country since independence had been religiously implemented, this country would by now outshine the United States in development. That is why I believe a true anti-corruption policy must involve the change from our present judicial system where the corrupt politician steals so much and is still deemed not guilty until proved. How? Why? This is rubbish. The thief has enough to bribes judges and goes scot free. We must change to the French adversarial system of justice where the accused is deemed guilty until he proves he is not. And we must incorporate the Chinese into our anti-corruption fight. They are experts. Bring them in and place them on commission. Merging the French and Chinese systems will see so much recovery of stolen and looted funds. A magistrate is presented with evidence, facts from a cleansed ministry of Justice or the EFCC or ICPC on a suspected politician. On the face of the facts, the accused is invited to give a statement on oath in open court. If what he is saying is so contrary to facts as to be sure he is lying, hand him over to the Chinese in the anti-corruption agency for interrogation. Before long, he will be telling you the ones he stole and those they didn't ask him. Much money will be recovered.

And I cannot be fully effective as governor if I don't clean up the Judiciary starting from the ministry of Justice. These state counsels frolic with criminals and their families, they get illicit money and throw away cases, stall cases, destroy the evidence they are supposed to use against the criminals and then the criminals are released back into society. By the time they have spent ten years in the ministry, they get a corrupt politician in a secret cult to back them and lobby that they be made judges. You therefore see very corrupt persons presiding over our justice system, wearing a robe, putting on a serious face and pretending to be righteous. Many are criminals and you wonder why the rot in society and in the administration of justice. I have detailed my attorney-general to carry out honesty tests on those state counsels and rid the place of the incompetent, the tainted and average lawyers. We want to employ fresh hands that are clean and want to work hard. They will be provided accommodation in heavily guarded compounds and with personal bodyguards. They will be on high pay to reduce incidents of temptations. By the time the Judiciary is working well, half of societal problems will be tackled. I have already liaised with the National Judicial Commission to help beam their searchlight on our judges and to root out those with questionable lives and judgments. The work of a judge should not be a reward for girl friends or for corrupt men in secret cults. And most of them belong to social clubs where they frolic with politicians and criminals. A Judge should live a secluded life, pouring over books not dancing disco. Reading some of the judgments of some judges is like something written by market women or expelled law school students. No philosophy, no insight, no intellectual stimulation. All this will change.

I am still exploring ways to set up an effective state anti-corruption body to primarily dig into all the budgets passed in this state since creation and get to the root of the matter and recover siphoned funds meant for public projects. All state and local government council budgets, all loans and grants will be given forensic scrutiny. Definitely, expatriates will be employed. They will uncover scandals and why all these failed projects that are everywhere. I am ready for the battle."

Governor Edeniyere established a new ministry of Budget Affairs to ensure the collation of all needed items to be put into the budget especially from the wards committees and to ensure budget implementation. An enabling law was passed to mandate that the state budget for the following year is submitted before the state House of Assembly not later than four months to the end of the current year.

He established a State Unemployment Relief Agency to undertake the enrollment of workers who can be available for public works, forestry jobs, the prevention of soil erosion, flood control and similar projects; to do a broad search into government departments to see existing vacancies and to create new vacancies; the arrangement for soft loans for artisans and other skilled vocations so as to expand their capacities; to run a farm Mortgage Scheme and a state Lottery Agency.

On inaugurating this Agency headed by Aimufua Obasohan, a former vice chancellor of the University of Benin and a professor of Sociology, he stressed that he was mandating them to declare war on unemployment and on whatever affects the purchasing power of the people. "Use your brain. Think", he told them. It was August 22, 2007 and the Nigeria House of Representatives faulted the award of N628 million contracts for the renovation of the official residences of the speaker, Mrs. Patricia Etteh, and her deputy, Alhaji Babangida Nguroje, and purchase of 12 cars.

Chapter 11
Waters over my soul

Governor Edeniyere continued his transformation of the state. Through his Industrialisation Policy, he set out to deliberately open up avenues for direct foreign investments across the state. Obaedo's dad was made the chairman of this state committee. He immediately set out to develop a close alliance with the Nigerian Association of Small Scale Industries and then with the state and federal chambers of Commerce, Industry, Mines and Agriculture to get ideas. Through his efforts, the administrative machinery of local government councils were harnessed to become liaison points for potential industrialists and entrepreneurs. Before long, dividends of his efforts started coming in as companies started flooding in. First to be given approval were companies with solar energy technology. The plan was to use the state as a springboard to solar-light up the state and then the country, starting from rural areas, lifting up the social and economic life of the people. Obaedo's father made sure the first company was sent to the governor's home village to commence operations. The entire village was lighted up on the night of the commissioning by the governor. He spoke about this new source of economic empowerment for better quality of life for the people that will spread to all rural communities. He also commissioned produced solar radio and chargers; solar lamps;

solar technology to provide hot water for rural populace; solar panels and other products.

"There will now be established Tourism Committees in all Local Governments Areas of the state to be headed by the local government chairman.", the governor said.

"They will identify potential tourist sites and encourage private sector participation for the development of tourism. This will generate local employment opportunities and foreign exchange earnings through international tourism. This solar power revolution today is only the start of much greater things for our rural communities. My friend Chief Ahamioje is certainly doing us proud. Before we came here, he briefed me on the readiness of our plans to float a company that will be public-private partnership to have thriving poultry and piggeries in every local government area. Jobs will be created, the rural areas will become more economic centres. Our state is open for business."

The crowd applauded.

....
....

Obaedo was gradually able to pull herself up and through the weight of the unfortunate incident with Nduka. She had borne the hurt and shame alone. She didn't tell the Bishop nor her brother and family what had happened because she suspected she might be blamed for asking for it by agreeing to travel with a young man alone. Nobody will believe her that he tricked her into travelling with him. Nor will they believe that she agreed to accompany him out of respect and politeness after she found out they were alone at the airport. Who will believe she didn't have her motives. Nobody will take her side against this very irresponsible boy. Certainly, Ifeyinwa will gouge out her eyes with blame, she thought. She remembered Sister Glory. Obaedo had kept away from church for a month. On the Sunday that she felt to attend, she went late and Nduka was leading songs during the worship service, shouting and bouncing all over the place. She kept her face down never looking up to the pulpit.

The Bishop came with his message. As usual it pointed to his special ministry. He would always back each sermon with voices he heard, "God told me", "The Holy Spirit said" and his experiences as of how the sun set when he was driving towards the eastern part of the city; how the wind blew into his study when he was reading Acts chapter 2; how he saw two doves set on his verandah just exactly at 9am on the 9th month of the year. Things like that. Today he was proving that he knows that as the apostles gave out the gospel, things men had not heard until then, his ministry will declare things never preached before. He read from the Bible Book of Deuteronomy, *Chapter 29:29 29 The secret things belong unto the LORD our God: but those things which are revealed belong unto us and to our children for ever, that we may do all the words of this law.*

Then he thundered out, "But it can't be a secret forever. Before Christ comes these things will be known and we will have a ministry to declare these unknown things, to which God will reveal them. Who will they be revealed to? These dead stiff preachers?" The congregation resounded with "No!"

Obaedo just sat and listened. After the service, some asked her about her absence and she made excuses. Her brother had also noticed her long absence and coldness but never pushing her, he didn't ask her anything directly. Back at school, Obaedo continued with her lectures and her Masters' degree programme. Her first year as a lecturer was over and the students had gone home for the holidays. She had not seen Billy since that day nor heard from him. He hadn't replied her email. She decided to go to his office one Saturday with a lunch pack from a fast food eatery.

Billy was surprised to see her as they were in their weekly law chambers meeting at the conference room. Billy's principal asked her to come in. He greeted her as Billy's friend. In all their womanizing and filthy talks about women which Billy never participated in, Billy had been different and never once ever brought a girl to the office. So they were all surprised to see a dashing young lady come visit him. Billy excused himself from the meeting and led her to his private office. It was small but cute with apt Scriptural and legal idioms engraved on beautiful pictures. The air-conditioner was working and his stock of books was impressive. Obaedo was proud of him.

"I just wanted to bring you this. It's been long."

"Thank you. The waters came over my soul."

"Me too."

There was a moment of silence. She saw Athol Fugard's classic, *Sizwe Banzi Is Dead* on his table and knew he had been reading it.

"But I know you will be okay. I am praying for you daily."

"I am relieved you look better Oba."

Hearing the pet name he alone calls her, brought tears to her eyes. She reached for her handkerchief. Billy waited for her.

"Are you going to be okay?"

She nodded.

Billy explained that he had to rejoin the meeting as they were strategizing on the cases for the coming week.

"Thank you for the lunch pack."

On rejoining the other lawyers, there was this wow! and murmuring.

Barrister Afolabi exclaimed, "I die."

The others went laughing.

"You mean you can attract a girl like this? Honestly man, I thought you were going to become a priest."

It was the head of chambers, the senior advocate and leading lawyer in town, Barrister Charles Ehizogie who put it perfectly.

"She is a real beautiful girl and one for keeps. You can just tell from her spirit that she is the homely type. Not those pretending ones. Billy, when your plans are coming up please let me know."

Billy nodded and the meeting went on.

Billy had not really given the thought of settling down. He was still a virgin! He took women as delicate things not to be played with as most men do. If she ain't yours, don't touch it; if you are not going to marry her, keep off; don't play with her feelings, were his private policy. He was billions of worlds apart from that egg-head who masquerades in the church leading the choir in the supposedly sole ministry on earth that revelations from God Almighty come to.

Chapter 12
Saving for my Queen.

Life went on for Obaedo. Time flew by. It became more than a year since that ugly incident in Lagos. She got some suitors in the church and in the university but she gave them no answer, keeping them in suspense. She started pondering if and when Billy was going to make a proposal. She liked him for he seemed like a father figure to her and her best friend. It would be any young woman's paradise to be married to him she thought. Altogether, he hadn't seen any man that compared to him even though she kept getting lots of attention from men. Mr Imade was a young lecturer in the Department of History and International Studies & Diplomacy {ISD} who also lived within her vicinity. He had before tried to be friendly with Ameze but he found that he just couldn't put up with her ways. Once he had called on her landline.

"It is Imade, please are you at home?"

"No, I'm in the market with the telephone cord around my neck."

He would sometimes drop by and give Obaedo hot snacks. He had once told Obaedo that he had a girl he wanted to settle down with but she was not really into him that much. One day when he visited her, Mr. Imade made a remark of her beauty in a suggestive way. It was like how the man who gets her will be real lucky. She eyed him and smiled. She then decided to start avoiding Mr Imade from then on. She avoided him until a day while she was about to go teach her class, just jotting some lecture notes on Ayi Kwe Armah's *The Beautiful Ones Are Not Yet Born*, Mr. Imade surprisingly came with an elderly man and a woman into her office. While he never looked up to her eyes, they both spoke on the wisdom of settling down. She never answered them a word until they got up and left.

Surprisingly, Nduka also visited her in her office that same day. They had not spoken to each other since the Lagos trip. She didn't know what to say to this unexpected visit, his barging into her privacy. Ameze who Obaedo had confided in on what had happened in Lagos was in her office when Nduka entered. She had been wild with anger like a bull when Obaedo had told her about the Lagos incident. Seeing him come to her office, the expression on her face was full of disgust. She has nothing but utter contempt for his person. She couldn't even bear saying a word to him. He was lower than the dust she thought.

"Obaedo, see you later," as she walked out stopping just short of hissing. She hated even the ground upon which this young man stood.

Nduka noticing the tense atmosphere, began by saying that he was most pained after the Lagos trip because he didn't know she had been a virgin. Although his father kept pushing him into the ministry he didn't feel that way. He told her his father was sending him to the United States for a convention to preach for him and he just came by to say farewell. Obaedo never once looked upon his face nor uttered a word to him. When he finally rose up to go, he said, "I miss us."

She went home later to ponder what he meant by "us". No doubt, he has repeated this same word to countless young women, in church and outside church she thought. "Nuisance," she muttered to herself.

Ameze would visit her at home later that evening and she told him of all Nduka had said.

"He is sly and despicable. You should allow me get my brothers in town to go arrange him. Oh yes. But he just can't come to see you. Heavens! There are some things people should never do. Just walk into your office after what he did? But who does he think he is? See how he walks in like an emperor. Has he no shame, no sense of decency? You are too nice Obaedo. But what are you doing with these people baby girl?"

Obaedo kept quiet.

"Look, you are too pretty and decent to be in the circle of this brute and those he represents. He is not your class.

Does he think just because you attend his father's church, a metaphor for the devil's playground, gives him a right to dominate your life?"

Ameze's face had contorted from her anger,

Obaedo smiled gently to her. "It is impossible not to connect with you Ame."

"Am being human Obaedo. I mean some people are so brutish. Taking advantage of a young promising woman, a precious life, because she stoops to attend your father's church and he is not even burying himself for years in shame but is still climbing the pulpit and still having the nerve to come to your office. I don't get it." Ameze was fuming, biting to her lip in anger.

They were both silent for a while.

"I hope he gets a near-death experience soon, shouting and begging for his life."

"Ame!", Obaedo was laughing loud. Her eyes were watery from the laugh. "O girl, you can give aspirin a headache."

"Yea, that is my only vice. A girl's virginity isn't for herself. It's for the man she will one day marry. It isn't for her to do as she pleases, to be squandered away to boys who say they love her but have no intention of making a vow unto her until death do them part. It's solely reserved for the man who will commit his life to her for all of his days on earth. It's for the man who wants to raise children with her and provide for her. She saves her virginity for this guy, a precious gift to him. And some church brute who ought to be rotting in hell will hide behind a pulpit and commit such heinous crime against a girl and against God, just take away something so precious to her, life's great asset to her? An underhanded brute who gets off only on detached sexual relief is going to mess up my girl and am going to hold back? No way. Obaedo, you are family."

"Thank you."

"Lure my buddy into unwanted physical intimacies and sexual violation. We are talking about forcing a precious young woman, subjecting her to sexual acts while she is physically helpless. And he's got the nerve to say he misses you. Real men consistently inspire respect in a woman not force their way on her or take advantage of her. Where are men with lives of integrity? These days especially these church ones, so immature and wishy-washy, all they do is strut on the pulpit, shout into a microphone and they expect all the girls to undress for them and am supposed to respect such? Claiming to be a Church whatever yet using deceptive strategies on young ladies, pretending to them, failing to take responsibility for their wrongs, controlling them with manipulation and mind games. Where is owning up to wrongs? Where is treating a lady like a precious gem that she is, communicating honestly with her that you love her and want her only, allowing yourself to be transparent and honest about who you are to her? If there's one quality in a man that will attract me, it is not masculine strength or pulpit oratory, it is to be stable. A guy who is calm-assertive, balanced, and consistently keeps his boundaries. Then he can add church to this. How can any real man allow himself to take a woman for granted, exploit her in the name of church? For a woman, when the conditions are right, she feels romantic; when the emotions are right, she feels sensual, relaxed, and open to a real guy. Deep down, every woman has certain repressed romantic desires that never go away. Really loving a woman will make her feel appreciated and she will want to reciprocate his love. It has nothing to do with manipulation. When I get ready to settle down, it won't be just because a brute shouts in the pulpit or attends church every Sunday. I want a charismatic communicator. A man who is able to use his words (and body language) to elicit favorable responses from me. Not pulpit manipulation or cheap tricks. Charismatic communication. Knowing how to lead a woman, to charm her out of her bad mood, he can verbally disarm her resistance (without firing a single shot), and leave her feeling safe—thereby making it easy for her to give him total and complete sensual surrender. Not taking advantage of her against her will. Communicating in a way that inspires her into a pleasant state of mind."

Ameze calmed down a little.

A film was playing on the DVD player, Tom Cruise as the protagonist in The Last Samurai; an American civil war hero, who had come over to join the ancient Japanese warriors, the Samurai and became a part of their cause.

"You know how to fight dirty", Obaedo told Ameze.

"I'd rather my brothers in town handle him. I'll save my dirty fighting for my hubby, when he arrives, whenever."

"He will never be able to get enough of you."

"Yea, I am chocolate."

"Sweetpea, no matter my mood, how my day is going, you are always fun to talk to."

"You are a shoulder to lean on too big girl."

"I'll always be here."

"Please let's talk something nice joor. How is your Oklahoma Hillbilly?"

Obaedo threw a chair pillow at her.

Obaedo continued to attend the Bishop's church. She had no conviction for this but just felt she should. Perhaps it was in being naïve or she just had a liking for the charm of the place, the same charm a hen feels for the hyena until it loses its life. The women's convention came and she was given a prominent role in several things including handling the Bible quiz. No matter her plea, Ameze declined to follow her.

One Sunday evening after church, there was a heavy down pour. Obaedo looked through her window to see a car entering her gate. It was her father. He had visited her few times before. He said he just came to check on her but she knew he carried a burden. He probed her on Billy and she wasn't sure on what to say. His counsel was as a young woman she needed to try settle down to avoid the avalanche of men's attention. He gave her some books he had bought during his recent trip to the States. She was so delighted.

Nduka had returned back from his trip and resumed his place in the church. One Sunday he was seen talking with Obaedo's brother after service. Obaedo wanted to know from her brother what it was all about. He just replied, "Marriage."

"You?"

"No, to you."

"But he can't be serious. What of Irene, Joy or Carrie that everyone knows about."

"I don't know. He was saying things about you."

"And what did you tell him?"

"Nothing, I was surprised."

Carrie showed her carnal female side the next Sunday in church after service even though she had led the special song of the choir that morning, *Jesus, You Are Everything To Me*. She hissed at Obaedo at the Car Park. Sensing something, Obaedo tried to ask her if there was anything wrong.

"If you don't know how to keep to your lane you will be hit girl," she said and stormed off.

Obaedo felt low. She went home moody despite just hearing a powerful sermon from the Bishop on the Biblical hidden Manna which only the high priest could receive. Of course that would be him today. On her way home, she had stopped at a fast food eatery to buy some snacks. She met some other sisters there. Some greeted but a few were cold to her unexplainably. She paid for her snacks and left.

To get things off her mind, she decided to call Billy. She told him what her brother had mentioned to her about Nduka.

"He is possessed and knoweth it not."

They chatted for about an hour and Obaedo felt lighter. Billy told her about his father's sermon that day on the Inviolability of Scriptures and tried to break it down.

"But doesn't the revelation of the Word of God come to

a man at a particular time", she asked.

"Yes, God sends a messenger in each period of time and to such a man He gives a notable ministry of His Word with outstanding divine backing. That man is designed from birth to catch the true Word for that period and lead the people from stagnation into a pure Move of God, a spiritual revival to turn back to God's ways. I learnt this pattern from reading the Old Testament and church history. However, until such a man comes in any age, who will be properly proven, we must stay with the Scriptures and their straight-forward plain meaning, imputing nothing of our own Ideas and impressions. By the way, if any man arises and then says things that don't fit in with the already given Scriptures, I just know that he is a false prophet and a charlatan. God does not do things outside the Scriptures."

"You sound just like your father."

"Should I sound like Bishop Azuka?"

Obaedo chuckled.

"I have found out that Satan has a counterfeit gospel, a pure imitation so real just like the real one. It is more flowery, sweeter and easier to receive. Although they talk of Christ, gather in His Name, preach from the Bible, have glorious feelings, they will still craftily introduce unscriptural teachings Christ never sanctioned into it. These human additions are destructive seeds and they eventually turn hearts from the Christ."

"Am listening", Obaedo said.

"This imitation gospel has a subtle beyond Bible limits as its rallying call. It can go outside the Bible to hold beliefs that are colourful and give great feeling. While the true gospel is unleavened, sane, in the middle of the road and will always stay within the Bible, remain at Calvary's feet and produce a decent Biblical-Christian life, Satan's is brighter and will never fully produce Christ in the people. His converts can go far but they cannot fully escape the corruption of this world and its system despite all their religious glamour and excitement because the seed of the Word of God to produce the Life of God is not in them. Just look at those Christian groups we saw on campus, rotten to the core. Have you ever wondered why a church and their man of God can seem to be riding the high waves for a season, be the talk of the town, with all the hype and noise but years later he ends up entangled in some scandal and godlessness. He goes down to zero while trying to hang unto his past glories. They didn't run with the Word."

"But why can't people detect it and walk away then?"

"It is not easy to detect. It is very subtle and can fool even the wisest of men. This counterfeit is a church system driven mostly by renown men but it is a parallel to that of

Christ. It is popular to the multitude and it is mostly what the people have known all their life as Christianity. They were born again by this church system and grew up in it. It is like their whole life and breath. They are sustained by this church which is like a life-support machine to them. To try to leave it will look like they are dying. So they quickly rush back to this their life-support. The peoples' allegiance is to this church system not to the undiluted Word of God. This is the reality."

"You sound convincing preacher."

"Oba, I still find time to study my Bible and the writings of true heroes of the Faith in past ages. This our day is full of so much counterfeit."

"You no doubt have our Bishop among your list of counterfeit."

"He is not really your Bishop. You are in wrong territory, I know you. You are better than that. Anyway I try not to pinpoint individuals as false Oba. I just watch what spirit rules men. I see what a man is trying to achieve; whether he is fading out, hiding himself, pointing people only to Christ and His life or if he is centering things around himself, making people to look up to him and his organizational empire. All Christian cult groups start from fanaticism and fanaticism is the refusal by man to be content with and humbly just come under what God has expressly given as His Word. That is how they all start. They think they are fired up. To a fanatic, he believes he is so inspired and undertaking a course which if God, according to him, knew all the facts, God would do same as he."

"If God knew all the facts?"

"Yes, that's how they think. It is laughable. This setting up of themselves to be operating on a self-imposed parallel frequency with the Almighty is at the heart of all Christian cult groups. They have pride and the audacity of rebellion. In a cult, there is suspension of doubts on the wild audacious claims by a man. No sense of irony in the fallibility of that man's heightened idolatry is felt. All safeguards against deifying a man are gone. Terror inevitably walks in into that House as the man continually resists accepting his own finiteness. The seed of this deception of false Christianity, this other seed after the first Sower Christ had sown His Seed, is sown deep into the hearts of people and they are then turned unto these powerful men in a most subtle way thinking they are following Christ but are actually following these men who are self-sent. The fruit is that these churches groups will be continually fashioned in the image and spirit of this man. The members consciously or unconsciously start to act like him, even to talk and behave like him. Then same sins that are in the world will start to become evident in these churches because they are merely following a man's spirit. Many have sunk in moral crisis. Real true healings have reduced. Salvation is reduced to just being a member of a church and attending its services. Church services major on feelings. This spirit upon people like your Bishop pretends to the people that it speaks by prophecy and not by his own rational conjectures. You see, it is human pride. It is deception. He makes people believe that his experiences, voices and sermons are by the divine rather than by his own human foresight. Such a thing can delude multitudes. In the Old and New Testaments, the Lord actually in a Body form or audible Voice spoke unto His vessels and whatever the Lord said unto a prophet or other chosen ones, that they speak out without addition, diminution or alteration. What is written in the Scriptures is enough for us and we don't need to embellish it or bring in new things. All these liars going about saying, "God told me," "God told me", a lying spirit is what brings new things apart from the plain Scriptures and it never deceives so deadly as in the mouth of preachers, false prophets. Millions are led off the cliff by so clever and an almost undetectable smart and deceitful craftiness, through a sleight of speech, a mental ingenuity that impresses and wows through smart, very nice and charismatic preachers. But anything that adds to God's given Word is a capital lie. You cannot add to perfection."

"Hmm. Your faith in the Bible is so strong. You blew me out."

"John Calvin said, 'There is no end to erring when we depart from the Word of God.' And this Word of God is the one from the very Mouth of God, the Scriptures, not the impressions of vain men. No, the Word of God in the Bible.

"I admire your convictions bro."

Billy laughed.

Obaedo was touched by his explanations. She pondered what it would be like to live with such a bright young man with godly wisdom and faith in God's Word. They talked further about their jobs. She unconsciously wanted to hear if Billy would hint at settling down soon. As they talked, Billy then mentioned how his father had spoken in the young men's group meeting of the need to become more responsible and start a family with a queen of their choice.

"He thinks it is easy to provide for a queen. My queen will get the treatment of a real queen. Stewards, servants, maids."

Obaedo laughed.

"Yes. If I have my way, I wouldn't want my wife to really work outside the house but be a real house wife. You know what Martin Luther said about couples?"

"What?"

" 'Let the wife make the husband glad to come home,

and let him make her sorry to see him leave.'"

"Sounds great."

"It is great. I like my wife to be house wife and perhaps be acting director of the private school I want to open. She will be at liberty to employ the staff and manage it but she will assign the day to day running to her employees. I will just be the pro-chancellor to come deliver 4-hours long graduation speeches. You know I will enjoy that a lot."

"I know you would baby."

They both laughed.

"You have great ideas."

"Yeah, I am nursing them. I will also borrow some from your father, ideas to open a poultry. You know how I love chicken."

"Will you allow any to mature and be sold at all? Seems you will always be visiting there to say, 'Give me 5 there, give me 2, give me 1.'"

"Right now, am enjoying my practice and getting to know a lot of influential men in society. At the same time, I am saving all my money for my queen. After all, there is no girl eating it from me now."

"Let me help you eat it."

"Thank you. I will take that under advisement."

She laughed.

"By the way I appreciate those two biographies of Franklin Roosevelt you sent to me from the collection your father gave you. Did you really have to do that? I am so grateful Oba. You needed to have seen me when I received them. I was intoxicated. If you had come yourself to deliver them, I would have lifted you up like a baby and thrown you in the air."

"You're welcome. Anytime Billy."

"Thank you Oba."
When they finished chatting, Obaedo was relieved and had so much fond thoughts about Billy. Later that night, she checked her email and saw a mail from Billy. There was no heading but it was a song by Whitney Houston, remixed a little by him.

Saving My Love For You.

A few stolen moments is all that we share

You've got your family, and they need you there.

Though I've tried to resist, being last on your list.

But no other woman's gonna do

So I'm saving all my love for you

It's not very easy, living alone

My friends try and tell me, find a woman of my own

But each time I try, I just break down and cry

Cause I'd rather be home feeling blue

So I'm saving all my love for you

You used to tell me we'd run away together

Love gives you the right to be free.

Obaedo was stunned. Is he implying what she has been thinking? She sighed continually because her words couldn't be formed. A lot of thoughts were racing through her mind. By 3am, she still had not slept.

Chapter 13
Dark Waters.

Billy was told that he had a visitor in his office one evening. It was Obaedo's father. He said he was in the neighbourhood and wanted to hand him a law DVD he bought for him during his last trip to the United States. It contained the constitutions, laws and decided cases of major European nations and of the United States Supreme Court. Billy was speechless. As he made to go, he asked, "How is my daughter?"

Billy was a bit caught off but said, "the last time we saw she was okay."

"You are sure? Well, at her age men will be bothering her a lot. I know she looks up to you as a friend and even a father. Do your best for her. She is a decent girl who will become her best when settled under a real man."

"I will try My best to ensure she makes her life worthy chief."

"That useless church she is going to, I hear a lot of rubbish goes on there, but finely covered up. Billy, nothing shows how brutish and nasty people can be more than in religion. I have nothing but disdain for them but she followed her brother Johnson there who up till now has not thought it fit to get married. A medical consultant? Isn't that a sign of sickness? Johnson has basically disowned me and his own mother because we refused to join into that crazy thing with him. He doesn't have any contact with us. Look, it is not even natural. Which Christianity from Jesus Christ will encourage you to despise your own parents? I've come to notice that there are certain traits that religious fanatics share; irrationality, stubbornness, being obnoxious, misquoting the Bible, willful ignorance. Some of the really nicest and most wonderful people I have known have been deeply religious but religion can do horrible evil. If being religious always meant a person would be warm and kind, I'd heartily recommend that everybody "get religion". It doesn't, sadly. They talk the talk, but rarely walk the walk. Children can become so stubborn, intractable, so closed minded. Thinking themselves wise, they became fools. These days, anyone that mounts the pulpit in church say that they are servants of God. But just because it looks like a duck, and quacks like a duck, doesn't mean that it is a duck. There are non-religious people that I have met and disagreed with and still went on to have an intelligent conversation with them. They are just very nice people. I admire them for their deeds, I enjoyed their company. But what my son has as his religion is an anti-social personality disorder, mostly exhibited by sociopaths and psychopaths. That church has taken over his brain you cannot even reason with him. He does not spend his money for anything else except for that place. He thinks I am lost and he possibly thinks you are too. But look at what he is. Is that the example he wants me or any responsible young man to follow? I am really tired of his life and I don't want that church to destroy my pet daughter too."

"Obaedo is fine sir. I am sure they cannot push her into doing things she doesn't want to do."

"But indoctrination and manipulation are very powerful and dangerous tools young man. Have you ever heard of the frog boiled slowly in cold water? That is it. You get so fascinated by these charismatic cult leaders and you are so overwhelmed by their presence till you can drink poison if they tell you. Women can just give in, lose their innocence so easily. Something women will fight off strongly if it were another person or place. But in these places, you don't think clearly and you just cannot break out and walk out. The truth with these charismatic cult leaders is that their lifestyle isn't as idyllic as it obviously seems to their deluded followers. They are experts, they have a hypnotic effect on people. Look at Jim Jones. He comes as good intention and meaning well but slowly it puts you into dark waters. I feel a strange and heavy wind. I fear for my daughter."

There was a rule in the Bishop's church that made certain number of sisters go to the Bishop's house at weekends to help his wife with household chores. The head deacon's wife made the arrangements. Nduka had also talked her into getting sisters to help him also with house chores. While she told her husband, many were not sure if the Bishop was aware. There have been gossips of sisters having tales to tell on such visits.

Nduka hadn't gone to his father to officially tell him he wanted to marry Obaedo but kept on with his flirtatious extra niceness. He would try chatting her up after choir practice, inquiring about her job. But Obaedo would be non-committal. While he was a university graduate of accountancy, he had constantly refused any kind of formal employment, mouthing that they cannot pay him. He inwardly detested being under any sort of authority and control, he loves being his own man. He lived on businesses, mostly getting supplies to companies. It is known that he is personally wealthy and his house so tastefully furnished.

When he called for a song practice of the choir in his house preparatory to the bishop's 65th birthday, Obaedo went for the first time. She was inwardly impressed by what she saw and what the young man had achieved for himself. Nduka was extra warm to her throughout the visit. In the middle of the rehearsal of a song, a young beautiful lady, Nkem, apparently a neighbor of Nduka, sauntered into his living room. She was casually but scandalously dressed in shorts that revealed a greater part of her thigh and just barely covering her modesty. She wore a spaghetti sleeves ladies' small top, revealing her navel and portion of her breasts. She left little to the imagination.

"Hi everyone. Sorry to intrude but Ndu I left my DVD here last night", she said in the borrowed accent of trendy girls.

"Is it Air Force One?"

Nkem eyed him playfully.

"Nope, Last Night in Vegas."

The way she chatted casually with him and her dressing left no one in that living room with a doubt that they had been intimate.

She collected the DVD and left. Some of the singers sighed. Carrie's face was sheer fury.

"Okay, where were we", as he resumed the song practice.
The following week, when the head deacon's wife told Obaedo that she was to go help Nduka with household chores along with Sister Faith, she agreed as a good church member would. She rested on the fact that since they were two of them, he couldn't possibly get any ideas. They went to Nduka's house early on Saturday. He opened the gate for them. He was having only his boxer shorts on. His chest was covered with

hair and the sisters modestly looked away as they greeted him. They cleaned up the kitchen, the living room and other rooms but stayed out of his bedroom. After sometime he came out, still in his boxer shorts and asked if they were not going to clean up his bedroom. As Sister Faith made to go in, he told her there were some clothes in the corridor he wanted her to wash. This left Obaedo to go tidy his bedroom. She entered and saw a tastefully furnished bedroom that hardly needed any cleaning. But she went on to cleaning the restroom. She saw copies of soft sell magazines in the restroom cupboard especially Playboy. She was not surprised. After being there for sometime, Nduka who had sat in the living room entered and put on the air-conditioner and an instrumental music. He lay down on the bed watching Obaedo do the cleaning.

"You know this might soon be your own bedroom."

She did not respond.

"Won't you talk back? Are you still angry?" He rose up to meet her.

"Please allow me do what am doing."

"But you came to my house and you just can't be so cold to me. When you are through, you will have to cook something special for your Bishop's son, before you go."

Obaedo said nothing.

His next action took her by surprise as he suddenly held her and drew her closer to himself. It was so sudden that before she could get her balance, he had placed his mouth on hers. She struggled to free herself but he hugged her from behind. She snapped out of his reach, shove him back and made for the door but it was locked. He came unto her again and was all over her. He proceeded to throw her against the wall and started aggressively kissing her face and neck. She was crying and begged him to stop. His eyes were wild and she was terrified and pleaded with him to please let her go but he was past caring as he suddenly threw her to the bed. She struggled but he was stronger and then she felt overwhelmed and weak as he was all over her. He breached her defense, crumbling her barrier of resistance and with the music playing loud, the air conditioner humming on, things went bad, again.

Sister Faith had finished and was waiting in the living room wondering why Obaedo hadn't come out. By the time Obaedo came out disheveled and moody, Faith immediately sensed what she feared.

"O! I am so sorry."

Obaedo never uttered a word as they both left.

Obaedo didn't go to song rehearsals later that evening or to service on Sunday. Nor did she go the following two Sundays. Who on earth will not blame her for this especially those she had confided in on what Nduka had done to her in

Lagos. For days, thoughts kept flooding through her mind. How did all this ever happen? Could all this have been stopped? Did it happen through the power of undue influence and respect for him and his father's ministry? Was her judgement impaired? Did it impact her ability to have truly read him all these while and interpret his true raw person and then make drastic decisions? Had it affected her capacity that morning not to have fought him off more wildly to a standstill? She was forced into a sex act as horrifying as it was, putting her in an emotional peril. Was she a willing participant in the sex act she was forced into, a horror show? No. Was she consenting? Consent cannot be given by a person who is incapacitated. She recalled his continual sexual harassment through flirtatious acts and advances, made by someone clearly in a position of spiritual power over her whom she respected. His pressure and suggestive advances ever since she came to the church had brought her confusion, shame and a reluctance to go public with it. Although she had once contemplated that in the car park she would one day shout him off to keep off her when she noticed he just kept working on her. But she feared the repercussions from the ministry; a ministry she had respect for.

Images of that Saturday morning kept on flashing through her mind. How he had groped her, fondled her, touching her inappropriately, exposed himself to her, and then forcibly had his way and it was all just something like, 'you're an animal, you're nothing, and I'm going to show you

you're nothing.' Peeling off and discarding her underwear like a candy wrapper, she remembered his vulgar expressions and lewd remarks that he had been burning to sleep with her again; on what her favourite position was. He had even called her a prude and also saying, 'you're not like the other girls', like if that was a compliment. But it only shows he doesn't even have any respect for the other girls he had messed up.

But did she give in to his sexual gratification easily? Why didn't she fight back like someone being mugged or robbed? Why did she not resist more? But women are conditioned not to use violence. Yes, many women's response usually involve aggressive resistance — even when the attacker is larger and stronger, suddenly they know 'kung fu'. But she had attempted flight, the door was locked; she even fought him within her strength but then she just later got weak, froze as he continued. She had screamed as she fought him but he was too strong and had pinned her down. He overpowered her. After her initial effort, she was rendered involuntarily immobile, becoming somewhat paralyzed as her brain and body just shut off. She just lay there. She didn't do anything; she was stiff like a board, almost like she was dead. He had been so violent, she just froze. It was almost as if she'd left her body and was watching this whole experience from 'outside'. She was in a state of shock. Tears were running down her face and he just did what he wanted to do and that was it, she had become an object to him, she was no longer a living, breathing human. Things had gone from somewhat the playful to confusing and terrifying, very quickly. The minute she had shove him off, his demeanor had shifted considerably. It was as if he was in "mission mode." When she had first kicked free, he followed her to the door. It was obvious that he had already decided that he was going to have sex with her and that she agreeing to come to his house was consent enough for him to do it. He had ignored her panic. It was like his body was on autopilot. She told him to stop, she said no, countless times. After no response to her desperate pleas, she resorted to whimpering, even crying. She eventually admitted defeat. He was strong, aggressive, and absolutely possessed. From that moment on, she was merely a device for gratification, rather than a whole entity, a lady. He shoved her face into the pillow and continued to have sex with her, pretending not to hear her. He had violently tore her jean skirt, breast holder and underwear and forced himself on her despite her efforts. She had kept saying no, as if it could restrain him, as if he'd magically stop it.

Her helplessness that morning would again return to her mind. How could she get have gotten this treatment from a ministry that she had believed in? She had not seen anything sinister in the request of the deacon's wife at first.... could she have said no to it, that she was not going when another sister would be there? What would her reasons have been? But going to the house of a man who had once violated her, she knew what that meant. To be alone with just another sister hadn't seemed enough. She had a bad feeling about it and had been apprehensive. Her gut had told her, 'You don't have to do this.' But her respect for the ministry won.

Obaedo sat up at nights for up to a week trying to process what had happened. The thought of going to the police felt painful to her. What would she say? Expose herself and her father to the ridicule of whole world? Who was she to even accuse a renowned Bishop's son of rape? She didn't know how to handle it at all. She was afraid she would be stigmatized and damaged more. She decided that she didn't want to go through the hassle of pressing charges. But should she have screamed louder? Fought him off harder? Had she been complicit in some way? All these questions raged through her mind. She would weep.

For days, she didn't talk to anyone, she couldn't eat, she couldn't sleep, didn't interact with anyone, not even the vibrant Ameze. She was too tired to speak, she was drained. She turned off her phone and for days would not speak. It was like she just bought a ticket to a planet where she lived by herself. When she eventually told her, Ameze at first just froze and then broke down crying. She hadn't seen her so broken before. Obaedo couldn't sleep at night without having a light on, because she had nightmares of being touched. In the seclusion of her room, she would scream. She felt lost and isolated from Billy. She saw Ameze hurting, deprived of her usual vivacity and joy. She thought of other sisters in church too that have been so abused. All of these things were extremely painful for her to contemplate and accept but what hurt the most was that her story was not unique. Many others young women have been violated by this Bishop's son who will just continue on with his life, thriving. She tried blaming herself for what had happened and internalized the guilt and shame that many women feel after sexual violence. But somehow deep within, she still felt she didn't deserve to be so violated in the way that she was. No one does.

When she resumed work after a week, she had to put on a good face. Everyone, including her colleagues and her parents, should never know how much like a slut she had been treated and debased. She tried pretending to herself that the whole thing wasn't real. She tried to push it out of her mind, but it was so heavy. At night, all her pain floated to the surface. It took her hours to fall asleep. She had assumed rape was a physical injury. She didn't account for the hollowing out of the mind, the loss of a woman's sense of self-worth.

Clearly Nduka had taken away her innocence, her worth, her privacy, her intimacy which she had vowed to reserve for Billy. He had taken away her confidence. The damage was done, no one could undo it. Her natural joy, gentleness and steady lifestyle seemed distorted beyond recognition. She became closed off, self-deprecating, tired, irritable and empty. The isolation at times was unbearable. It was like nobody could give her back the life she had before that Saturday morning. The experience had terrified and traumatized her to the core. It left her feeling ashamed, embarrassed, dirty and alone. The young man had left scars on her for life. Her childlike innocence of loving to go to the Bishop's church had brought her into dark waters. Church had become a place where she had met a man as evil as nothing she had ever met. It's people like these that make women hate men and make others turn on God.

The biggest shock of her life came three weeks later. She started feelings drowsy and weak especially in the mornings. When it persisted, she attempted to take malaria tablets on her own but decided to see a female consultant friend at the University of Benin Teaching Hospital, UBTH. The signs she told the consultant made the consultant to look deep into her eyes. Obaedo couldn't explain what the look meant. Dr. Emily Okpaise didn't want to intrude into her personal life but felt compelled to ask of her love life. Everyone knew Obaedo to be pretty decent but you couldn't be too sure with women as the number of cases she has had to deal with.

Obaedo stopped in her thoughts. Looking straight to Dr. Okpaise, she said "I understand."

By the time she did the pregnancy test, it was positive. Obaedo was consoled by Dr. Okpaise who knew her well that this must have been a big mistake on her part. She further spoke nice words to her knowing she wouldn't think of an abortion.

"Am sorry to ask but am sure you know the father?"

"Yes."

"Come here, you need a hug. Please I will call on you later at home this evening so we can talk. Don't be too hard on yourself please."

Chapter 14
Heart of a slave.

Governor Edeniyere had commissioned a first class fruit juice production company at Ehor near Benin City in partnership with a South African firm. The state government provided the land and necessary infrastructure but conceded majority shares and management to the private company. Harnessing the fruit resources of the state, he said that this production company will see more jobs created and revenue will accrue to the state from this joint-venture. He had also launched three Senatorial mechanised farms with an Israeli firm. Keeping his promise to provide more educational opportunities, the State Institute of Practical Engineering and Artisans was constructed and opened in collaboration with a Togolese firm. As governor, he had turned the state into a massive construction site. Many of the state capital roads were expanded and given street lights at night through solar energy.

When asked what was his driving force, he had said, "I travel a lot overseas and believe you me I always want to reproduce what I see and enjoy over there right in my home state. It is a personal conviction. Look at how the chairman who ran our transport company JAGUAR aground and has been attacking my administration. This man uses the title 'Deacon' and he is a saint. Everyone in this state knows how satanic-corrupt things were under him even depriving pensioners their entitlements through fictitious practices. If a man who carries church on his head cannot be motivated to act right, to do the right things, we are in trouble. Also I am aware of millions of naira he gave out to leading Bishops in this state just to curry favour to be prayed for. Which God will answer prayers for a thief? Please tell me. I am not going to bother recovering those money from those church leaders. If they are okay to lie to their conscience and receive money that everyone knows is stolen, let them keep and eat it. I move forward on my convictions to develop our state."

....
....

Johnson, Obaedo's brother was especially cold in the church officers' meeting, called by the Bishop after Obaedo had told him of her condition. Present were the Bishop, his wife and the domineering Ifeyinwa who sat with her legs crossed and a sarcastic look on her face. The church deacons and their wives, Nduka and some church elders were also present.

The Bishop as usual wanted to rub off on girls that cannot be decent and keep themselves, throwing themselves after men and suffering bitter consequences. Ifeyinwa gave a mock smile to this. Obaedo just sat expressionless, bottling up all the insults and insinuations. When Nduka was asked to speak, he halted with his words that he cannot understand why Obaedo would put this on him. Obaedo was pondering why no one had directly asked Nduka that very pertinent question if he had slept with her. The overbearing presence of the Bishop was well known and all of his officers never said anything contrary to his views. Certainly not in the presence of Ifeyinwa. Loyalty to his person, a vacuous loyalty, had been deeply engrained in them and this was one virtue they all tried to maintain. Bishop Azuka's authoritarianism was equated with leadership and to dissent was taken as apostasy. The system had left no room for choice, no room for free will nor for exercising basic intelligence of man. And when men cease to think for themselves, they cease to exist as humans. These men would do most anything to defend the Bishop and the church. Defending Bishop Azuka was not limited to his officers but other churches as well where his influence has been cast, gave him blind loyalty. They were strangely drawn to his person and ministry. Most of them would only take a meaning of the Scriptures as Bishop Azuka taught it. These pastors who hold him as an apostle will never take most any private or spiritual decision without first travelling down to seek audience with him and get his input. It is also true that the Bishop can be devilishly vindictive and had successfully used his influence to break up several congregations across the country and support a factor with resources to fully establish another ministry. Of particular note was The Good Shepherd Assembly in Ughelli, Niger Delta Nigeria, where the Pastor, Chuka Ezeh, was known to be a fierce critic of the many outlandish claims of Bishop Azuka. Pastor Ezeh's assistant, Minister Mike one Sunday just entered the pulpit and strongly rebuked Pastor Chuka for speaking against an anointed servant of God in the person of Bishop Azuka. He then called for a vote from the congregation to remove their pastor. A stunned Pastor Chuka, came out from his study and confronted his assistant. It almost became physical but by the time hostilities calmed down, more than 80% of the congregation had walked out with the assistant pastor. It later emerged that Minister Mike has been a constant visitor to Bishop Azuka surreptitiously. On setting his own church, he notably invited Bishop Azuka for the dedication.

"Young girl, you will have to search your heart to know if you are sure of your allegation. Because this can be very damaging to this ministry", one of the deacons said.

Obaedo kept quiet.

Others spoke but none dared ask that very question.

Ifeyinwa then asked Obaedo a particularly embarrassing question of if she had not lost her innocence before she started attending their church. She didn't reply. To which the Bishop said he was calling off the meeting.

It was at that moment that the head deacon James Nnayelugo, who had remained silent all along said he wanted to say something.

"My wife had told me years back how Nduka approached her to periodically arrange for sisters to come help him with his house chores on Saturdays. I didn't like the idea and told her to ensure two or more sisters went at a time. I remember telling you Bishop Azuka about it but you gave me no reply."

The Bishop adjusted in his seat.

"I watched how Sister Glory was literally disgraced out from this church because she told my wife of the sordid thing that happened in that house, things that shouldn't be mentioned among us Christians, when she went with Sister Chika to Nduka's house. No one seemed to believe her. I wasn't man enough to stand with her then."

"Where are you going with all this?" blurted out Nduka.

"Calm down, let him go on", Bishop Azuka replied.

"Thank you Bishop. What I am saying is that for some time now, this ship has been going into uncharted waters. I feel we have been leaving a solid foundation of the Bible, dabbling too much into feelings and this House is shaking. Things like this prove what I am saying. I believe Obaedo Ahamioje. I have watched her since she first came to our church. She is a decent and properly brought up girl. Look at her now. Is there anyone here who will swear on the Holy Bible to say that this young promising lady who will even get suitors from Princes around the world would just throw herself into an unstable young man's bed just to lose it all? For what? To bring such shame upon herself for nothing? Please read her motive. Is she making these so-called 'wild allegations' in revenge? Why would she do that? Is she full of hate or out to get at this ministry? Please get your facts right before you judge. She is still calm after finding herself in a most embarrassing situation. How can she now face her colleagues, her friends and her family? Will life ever be the same for her? Please how we handle her here might determine her future. We must put personality aside and be Christians in deeds not just in rhetoric."

That was one word the Bishop hated that many of his critics use to describe his ministry. His face grew stiff. Ifeyinwa looked at her father. Deacon Ugo continued.

"This shame has not just come upon her, but upon this ministry. We need to deal with it maturely. I don't think she is a wayward girl or the type of girl who will go for abortion because she could have. If I may say, I have heard gossips of her being another of Nduka's desire for marriage. But how many sisters will a young man run after to marry? Well, it is known that Obaedo was not chasing after him like many. Being a subject of affection of a Bishop's son can make many girls to swell up and give in easily but it hasn't even got to her as to make her proud, arrogant and wanton. I don't know if it is her decision to agree to Nduka's proposal. So why would she do this to trap Nduka in marriage. I think she is a victim and simply wants things straightened out.

What she told my wife, I heard also from sister Faith who gave a picture of what happened. Why would Nduka insist on a young lady cleaning his bedroom alone and locking his door? Brethren why? People will say, 'Why did she not cry out or fight him.' She told me she did but that he locked his door and she got overwhelmed by his excesses. Yes, it is partly a female problem, being touched like that. It is also partly being overwhelmed by undue estimation of men. I have been disturbed lately about how people have been over exalting this ministry, raising it up as God to the extent that some are ready to kill for our Church. A young girl in this atmosphere may find herself not being able to be very firm and rude and to turn down flatly such carnal demands from someone so exalted. Infact she won't be thinking clearly. It is undue influence. So to attack her alone, is not Christianity. Obaedo told me she became weak in resisting him. I scolded her in not attacking him more fiercely but she told me with tears that she tried her best. Usually when a woman is called into the bed of a prince, my fellow men, we all know only few women in the world would storm out. It is not just in all their make-up. I do not think Obaedo would have even answered Nduka's call. But she was not even called, she was unduly coerced into doing what is a sin, a crime against the laws of this country was committed."

"You mean rape?", another deacon asked him.

He didn't reply. Continuing Deacon Nnayelugo said,

"Nobody here knows but she told me that this is not the first time. He had lured her into travelling to Lagos with him under the guise of inspecting church equipment and then defiled her last year, he took her virginity."

There was low murmurings.

"Out of fear she kept quiet and told nobody. It was only this week she confessed it to me. To castigate this young lady with a bright future who has been dented deliberately and wickedly, is a sin against God and mankind. Take a good look at her. Who here in his heart of hearts except the depraved heart of a slave, a worshipper of a man, can say that Obaedo is just making this up? That she invented all this? Truth is a powerful thing, it cuts. Are we now saying this Obaedo is another sleep around church girl who got her dues? I say nonsense. Nonsense! I totally believe what Obaedo said happened that Saturday morning at Nduka's house."

There was an eerie silence in the room. Obaedo was

wiping her eyes with her handkerchief. The expression on Nduka's face betrayed his guilt.

The Bishop spoke, first slowly. "I am not surprised at what you have been saying, taking sides and believing wild allegations to smear my ministry. For some time now, I've been watching you in this church. You think you know more Bible than me. Perhaps it is your will to take over this ministry."

Deacon Ugo smiled to himself.

"I will not allow strangers come in here and destroy what God has taken years to build. I will not stand by and watch devils throw smut on my family or on my ministry. Not in my church. My ministry is known not just in this nation but across the world. God has vindicated it and proved its place. Thousands look up to it around the world because it is a life source to them."

"Christ the Word of God is our life source not a ministry", Deacon Ugo interjected.

"Shut up your mouth! Don't you ever speak while I am talking. You keep quiet and listen!", the Bishop shouted.

"By next Sunday, I will announce to the church that you are no more head deacon of this ministry. And if I find you causing any schism, I will handle it in a way you will regret.

You wouldn't believe the things you will see from me. Try me."

Deacon Ugo's wife, Ifeoma fell down on her knees imploring the Bishop.

Deacon Ugo reached her by the hand, "Honey, let's go."

They left and never returned.

Outside, Obaedo's brother could only castigate her for the shame she had brought upon herself. At the Car Park, many looked at her with eyes between pity and shame. She entered her car and drove off.

The next Sunday service was titled, War in Heaven. It was dedicated to 'casting out whoring lying sisters in the mode of Jezebel sent by Satan to infiltrate spiritual Israel.' There was a visiting minister, Pastor Onyekulum who was to bring the day's sermon. Bishop Azuka had reserved the right to choose what he called God called men, ministers who stand with his self-proclaimed apostolic calling and commission. These five-fold ministers as he also called them, although pastors of their own congregations were in a brotherhood with him and usually preached at his convention meetings and regularly visit his church to preach. They all most always just mouth things the Bishop loves to hear, satisfying his itchy ears. It would appear the benchmark of their sermons was the Bishop's approval and not their deep down convictions of the Word of God. So they just most times regurgitated the Bishop's own sayings, echoing back all his rubbish and buttressing his claims of being an apostle. Many of these ministers had been handsomely rewarded by him through the years. Some have been sponsored on overseas trips; some were allowed to marry choice sisters from his church and others have continued to receive huge financial assistance from him. Some have fallen out of favour with him and he had then declared to the congregation with hot anger that they are no more five-fold ministers.

Ifeyinwa the Bishop's daughter was especially fond of one of these pastors, a young man, Pat Chimezie of the Light House Mission at NIFOR near Benin. Whenever the young preacher visited her father's church, she would been seen smiling ear to ear and be all over him chatting even though she was ten years senior to him in age. It was rumoured that Ifeyinwa would have jumped into marrying him at this time had the young man not been already married. Infact Chimezie was said would have been her real heart's love and husband, not the one she had married for his wealth. It is known that she visits him at his work place at NIFOR, bringing him delicious dishes and other gifts. The Bishop knew all these but turned a blind eye to it. Once Ifeyinwa had bought the young preacher a birthday gift with a card which his wife had seen and came crying to show the Bishop. The card had read:

'Sometimes, you can't explain what you see in a person, it's just the way they take you to a place where no one else can. Texting is fine, calling is okay, but being with you is the best. I am a strong person but every now and then I also need someone to take my hand and say everything will be alright. Two things people should never have to chase; true friends and true love. They find us. I want to sleep with you so bad. I don't mean have sex. I mean sleep together, under my blankets, in my bed, with my hand on your chest and your arm around me. Not talking, just sleepy, blissful silence.

Happy Birthday my chum.

Ify.

It is reported that when the Bishop tried to interrogate her on the card, Ifeyinwa had reacted angrily and walked out making the Bishop to burst out into a loud and long laughter, rolling on the floor, holding his ribs and mockingly repeating some lines from the card…'I want to sleep with you but I do not want to have sex with you. *Odiegwu*'. He would burst out again into another round of loud cracking laughter. Ifeyinwa's mother was not amused.

Pastor Chimezie has a very handsome face and is very calm with an easy smile. It is said that he has a way to make Ifeyinwa filled with fun, happiness and to show her tender femininity. Everyone knew about her life and stress as a single mother, Pastor Chimezie is the one person with whom she can let her guard down. She had told her mother that Pastor Chimezie is the one person that she can afford to be real to and be open to, telling him her weaknesses without shame and getting counsel. She even tells him things that she had done and is not proud of and that she regrets. Looking at Ifeyinwa when she is chatting with Pastor Chimezie, people see glowing from her a softness, a tenderness, nurturing and a sweet side that they rarely see in her. She would just look like a girly girl! After chatting long with him in the church basement after church service, she would escort him to his car and still lean over against him on the car, talking with him before he drives away. On a day when it had rained, she escorted him to his car, holding an umbrella over both of them. On such days, she would be so enlivened as to smile freely and exude a peace from within. She constantly communicates with him by text messages. While she always surprises him with gifts, especially books, he has a special way of teasing her that no other person would dare. If there is any one person that treats her like a princess, it is Pastor Chimezie.

There were two prominent ministers among the lot who were the closest to the Bishop. One was Pastor Abbe of Life Camp Akure. He out-did others in trying to prove the acclaimed apostolic ministry of Bishop Azuka and of his devoted loyalty to their brotherhood. Outwardly looking refined with the disposition of a peasant, he lacked the 'hell fire' preaching spirit of the Bishop but had a taste for scholarlistic preachings. He dotted his sermons with Biblical latin words and their meanings, using penetrating analysis and an unhealthy romanticism for strange and mysterious teachings. He was the brotherhood's in-house theologian and was mostly responsible for spreading the ministry of the Bishop far and wide. He could be an energetic publicist when it comes to the ministry of the Bishop. He however lacked the Bishop's originality but he had a very fertile imagination. His favourite lines include, "For years my ministry was stagnant, I literally had nothing. I found here a home, a family and spiritual and financial stability in this brotherhood of our apostle. If any of you walks out you will lose your lifelong identity, your only known community, and you will lose the ability to be sure of anything anymore not to talk of entering into financial ruin. This ministry has sustained us all spiritually and financially."

Outside the pulpit, he cut the figure of a mediaeval ecclesiastic and looked like he would have made a successful career as a tour guide.

The other minister was Pastor Christopher Onyekulum of Sapele. Tall, dark and dry with a rigid piety, he is energetic with a slow arrogance. He preaches with a rancor and bitterness not found elsewhere. Many might take him for an anti-clerical fanatic the way he raves at ministers who don't believe in the brotherhood led by Bishop Azuka. His sermons never wander far from sex devils and ministers and his words often degenerate into hardcore expressions freely used in brothels and not supposed to be used in a mixed audience. Known to be selfish and to quarrel often, he is a genius for destroying the reputation of others. Absolutely self-possessed, he would often say, 'We are uncovering dark secrets of the ages.' 'I was born a preacher, no man called me.' It was like he saw an opportunity to become renown by associating with Bishop Azuka and did not fail to profit by it. His propaganda on behalf of the Bishop was of an elevated type. The Bishop had invited him during the week to come minister, telling him of what was on ground. The Bishop knew what a good hired gun he could be in character assassination.

Before the visiting Pastor Onyekulum came to speak this day, Bishop Azuka first came to the pulpit. The Bishop went from shouting to actually raving that a medical doctor brother, Dr. Ohimai, later said he feared he might have gotten a heart attack.

"If you cannot be under my revelation, my revelation, what God gave me for this day, you can leave! I invite you to leave! But I know who met me, who anointed me and commissioned me and who have vindicated me all these years. I have the Word of the Lord for today. To me it is given to open your understanding of the Word! The great signs and miracles that have taken place under this ministry proves its special place on earth. Where else do you have a ministry which the truth of the Word is opened to? Where? It is unthinkable that those I brought up from the gutter, those who were once jobless but for my continuous welfare assistance to them and their family will now align with wanton Jezebels to attack my family, malign my son and try to destroy this church that has the Word for this day. The apostle Peter was God's spokesman for his day. God has a spokesman for this…'

His words were drowned out by the frenzy and shouts from the congregation.

The young medical doctor, Dr. Ohimai was not moved by the Bishop words. He sat down moody while the Bishop raved on and even when the whole church exploded in an emotional bout. He was also deeply offended by the reckless use of unprintable words by Pastor Onyekulum clearly targeting Obaedo that at a time during his sermon he was so tempted to rise up and go confront him openly.

Dr. Ohimai had nursed a desire to one day get married to Obaedo. A very successful Consultant in General medicine, he too had been drawn in by the Bishop's charisma. However lately, he had been getting uncomfortable with the centre of every service and sermon being the person of the Bishop. He once remarked to Johnson that in one particular month, the Bishop never mentioned "Christ", or "Our Lord" or "Our Saviour" in any of his messages. It was all about himself. Johnson had then replied that Christ was now veiled in the Bishop, misquoting the Scriptures, 'If you see me, you see the Father.' Dr. Ohimai was however not impressed by this explanation. He had watched Obaedo and really liked her. He was shy whenever they met at the car park to exchange greetings. He was not the bold type to cross a lady's lines. He bided his time. When he had heard that Obaedo was pregnant, his spirit was killed. He knew Nduka was not a Christian by conversion but just a nominal one who to him were the most dangerous species on earth. If he was a nonbeliever out there in the world, everyone would know him thus. But to be an unconverted and masquerade himself in church as a saint and even dare to go behind the pulpit, was a most unforgivable sin. He had a female neighbor who was living with a married man who was into the notorious advanced fee fraud. But the whole neighbourhood is woken up each morning by the loud religious church singing of this woman. Dr Ohimai's spirit is always vexed to its extreme when she starts singing. To him this was the same spirit in Nduka, a religious enterprise that has nothing but earthliness attached to it. His religion scorns the way of the true Cross and his worship while loud and glamorous, lacked the reverence of a heartfelt religion. It is a sickly thing born of the union of a heart of worldliness with a head of knowledge; a bastard thing with a lost church as mother and the world as its father. And only a depraved unconverted heart of a minister will produce such and accommodate such in his ministry.

He sat in his car and watched as Obaedo drove away after the church service. Tears welled up in his eyes as he considered her plight. Of all the people that this ministry had destroyed, Obaedo's treatment provided the best depiction of the Bishop's satanic church system. He put his head on his steering wheel, thoughts racing through his mind. 'This church has been like cholesterol blocking the flow of my blood. All it has achieved is just sucking people into the abyss. We have been so brainwashed that we really believed this man's unscriptural claims. Some of the nicest, most giving people I have met in life come here and have just got sucked in, chewed up, and swallowed into the abyss. This clever Bishop sped down the path of feel-good impressions, never minding the plain Scriptures. The spirit of error, the anti-Christ spirit is so feel-good, a sensation-giving, so enlightening, tears-in-the-eyes religious feeling. You just feel so right and secure. But watch it closely, it is subtly off the pure plain Word of God which is the Spirit of Christ. The mantra here was: adulate Bishop Azuka, embrace his every revelation, and submit to his complete leading and you are saved. In this excitement and rush, precious lives were placed on a crash course of ruin.

It is time to end this. I am a little too old to be associated with such idiocy! Continuing to be here is inexcusable. You know you're a disgrace when Bishop Azuka and his son are pastoring you.'

Then like the feel of a sting, a thought had come to him. He sat back. He knew a lot of innocent girls who just snapped from such huge strange experiences in life. First they feel banishment, followed by dissolution, then wandering, finally darkness falls on them. He began to fear for Obaedo.

News of Obaedo's pregnancy spread. Her father took a heavy blow with the news of his daughter's pregnancy outside wedlock. Worst still that the man had denied paternity. He felt ashamed like never before. His thoughts wandered from using armed thugs to go invade the Bishop's church one Sunday, thrashing the whole place; to disowning Johnson. But his wives calmed him and invited Obaedo to come home. They spent time consoling her and giving her advice, praising her for her decision not to abort the baby. She said little. Her mother was heartbroken and pained. Obaedo stayed at her fathers' house for three weeks, receiving great emotional support. Ameze was a regular visitor to see Obaedo at her father's house.

"That young man must have a death wish. I knew it the first time I saw him, his cold eyes", she said grimacing on one of her visits. Obaedo would just lie down saying nothing.

"What a grossly irresponsible young man with terrible satanic values. How can they do this to a decent, educated, attractive woman?" She asked to nobody in particular. "What sort of people will do this and deny responsibility? How does messing up a radiant life translate into Christianity of any sort? Look at the church cultist David Koresh, having sex with other men's wives and preaching celibacy to their husbands. This wicked spirit used mind manipulation to reduce his fellow men into zombies who would follow his teachings without any recourse to reason or according to the course of nature. Which religion or God will sanction you taking another man's wife yet men were made to accept this practice and still followed that damned pervert. The same thing with Jim Jones. These megalomaniacs hold out to be representatives of the Almighty but they so bend the people to follow only their wish and not to think for themselves nor to question their authority. They tell lies in the name of God and have no conscience to prick them. As the FBI confronted Koresh to come out from his stronghold, he first agreed and later he told them that God told him to wait. Which God? Obaedo, my hat is off to your gentleness. How you do it I never know. You are special and unique. I wouldn't question your judgment in going to that church in the first place; you had no doubt good intentions. But doesn't this cross the line? In this world my sister, a lot of people were born wicked. They are pathetic. Expecting them to treat you decently because you are gentle and good is like expecting a bull not to charge you because you are a vegetarian. You need a fresh break. I know you will and will come through this, stronger, I know. You are not alone."

Billy had taken it all with a serene calmness. No one knew how he heard but he found his way to Obaedo's father's house where she was staying. The family had left the two of them alone in the living room when he came. They sat in silence for close to the space of half an hour. Billy was reminiscing on their secondary school days, the many precious times that they had spent together in this living room. It was an innocent beautiful world then.

"I know you are going to keep the baby", Billy broke the silence.

Obaedo eyes were streaming tears, she said nothing.

"Well, I know you will."

Tears welled up in his eyes and he rose to leave. Obaedo was now sobbing freely, uncontrollably.

Still awake at 2am, he sent her a text message. She had a feeling he would.

I've spent a lifetime saving my best for her. She made me cry but I won't ask why. It never was in her to. Am hurting. But I know she is hurting more. Don't try to explain because words are never enough. We had the greatest love beyond words. It was pure love, nothing more, nothing less. We had all the time in the world to birth our own new world, to unfold precious things. Take heart. Time is a healer. I will always love you.

Your Bill.

When she had to move back to her own apartment, her mother went with her and stayed with her for a month. By this time, her father had arranged for a young girl, Anita, to move in and be her maid. She bore all the reproach and slanderous innuendos of an unwed pregnancy in the university and among her friends and colleagues. She bore it all. As time went on, she would once in a while attend the Bishop's church for reasons no one could explain. Perhaps she was trying not to get hardened by staying away from church services or it was just to prick their conscience. However, this was one place she had always loved going to before the unfortunate experience. Those days that she came to service, Ifeyinwa answered her greeting coldly and the Bishop behaved as if she was not there even though he must have seen her in the balcony. He carried on with magnifying himself above the stars of God- that nobody else can provide the meaning of the Word of God except what came to him in his experiences and voices. Obaedo would sit in the balcony and just observe the services, barely showing any emotion.

One Sunday service, something took place that would later add to the complete unraveling of this religious foundation she had stood on for long years of her life. She had come late as usual and to her surprise the service was not going on. It was rowdy inside the auditorium. There was a black American family and their friends at the top of the commotion. What came out was that a daughter of a black

American preacher named Bethany, had become pregnant ostensibly by Nduka. During his trip to the United States to represent his father in that convention, he had gotten intimate with the minister's daughter and lured her into fornication throughout his stay. The American preacher had told Bishop Azuka when his daughter became pregnant but he had denied on his son's behalf. Now after delivering a baby boy that was clearly in Nduka image and despite pictures sent to the Bishop, he still defended his son. Now the American family travelled down to Nigeria to create a scene and make a point. There she was, Bethany, a beautiful young black American girl and her mother quietly observing the melee while the males exchanged words at the top of their voices. Obaedo was further broken. And to think that when Nduka returned back from that trip to the States, he had approached her brother Johnson on marriage to her. 'What a monstrous wolf amongst humans,' she sighed.

As she got heavier, she still went few times to the services with Anita. Back at home, she would engage her in lively conversations as if she were her little sister. It helped because gloominess started melting away from her heart. Billy visited her some weekends and kept up with emails and calls. When her expected date of delivery finally came, August 1, 2009, Obaedo gave birth to a baby girl at the University of Benin Teaching Hospital. Her mother again moved into her apartment. She had wanted to have her baby dedicated in the Bishop's church. Although she passed this request through a deacon to the Bishop, she never got any reply. Nor did the ministry even visit her after it was known she had delivered. Some individuals in church including Sister Faith came to visit. When she saw Obaedo, she broke down in tears.

Obaedo took the silence from the Bishop as a 'No' to her request. The pain and shame of rejection, once again, overwhelmed her but she slowly regained strength from the constant stream of visitors, including her students who made her a custom-made large congratulation card. Many of them wrote nice little messages on the card.

Chapter 15
Breaking Point…Dawn.

Perhaps Dr. Ohimai was right. People reach their tipping point. As soon as Obaedo was strong enough to start work, her maid Anita, kept the baby and the home front for her very well. She adapted well both as a mother and a career worker. She still retained her dashing looks and the smiles gradually returned. A lot of her friends had gotten over her reproach and had come in torrents to see her and cheer her up. Ameze, who had gone to London on a scholarship for her doctorate programme, kept calling, cheering her up. They all knew now that she had been a victim of a monstrous evil. But deep in her heart, Obaedo still felt something was missing. Was it that original fire that she had with Billy which had somewhat almost burnt out with just few flickers left? The innocence they had shared together along with his warm company now seemed distant. She couldn't really place it. But her life's block seemed broken. She had been deeply hurt by the whole incident of the pregnancy and the follow up by the Bishop, especially his declining the dedication of her baby. "Is this Christianity, the thing I gave my life to?" she would sigh.

Sister Faith had visited her once and told her of another sordid incident in the Bishop's church. Nkem, the neighbor of Nduka had stormed the church with her family to raise hell on Nduka pregnating her and denying paternity. Obaedo just sat and listened, muttering words to herself.

While Ameze was in London and she still called, Obaedo really began missing her person and company around home. She was not herself. She remembered Oscar Wilde, 'Some cause happiness wherever they go; others whenever they go.' Happiness was wherever Ameze was; she was a constant source of it. What a girl, she sighed. Obaedo needed at this time what only she could provide and her absence was making her feel very miserable. Some nights she would just sit up and cry. Loneliness, it seemed, just wouldn't leave her alone. She recalled some lines from George Awoonor-Williams' Songs of Sorrow:

> *Dzogbese Lisa has treated me thus*
>
> *It has led me among the sharps of the forest*
>
> *Returning is not possible*
>
> *And going forward is a great difficulty*
>
> *The affairs of this world…*
>
> *My people, I have been somewhere*
>
> *If I turn here, the rain beats me*
>
> *If I turn there the sun burns me*

She found herself many times echoing Cardinal Wolsey after he had been sacked by King Henry VIII:

Had I but served my God with half the zeal

I served my king; He would not in mine age

Have left me naked to mine enemies.

One nagging thought she kept battling with was whether she and Billy will ever return to that innocence they once had; that thing that just bonded them. When the university therefore chose her as a member of the team for a World Bank two-week workshop in Abuja, organized for bright young lecturers, she thought this her opportunity to get some fresh air and get her groove again.

They were all lodged at the Hilton Hotel Abuja, promising young male and female lecturers from many African and Caribbean nations. She was given her own hotel Suite. She met and became friendly with other dashing young lecturers, male and female. After the day's working sessions, they would all tour different parts of the federal capital in the late evening. On returning to their hotel, they would converge around the swimming pool area and bar, just chatting away. Obaedo was finding relief.

A young lecturer from Jamaica, Dr. Glenmore had taken keen interest in Obaedo. He even would comment openly on her beauty and sit next to her in the bus that took them on the city tours. He would be around her at the swimming pool area chatting about his country and his field of specialty. Obaedo somewhat liked his person. He would escort her to her room door when they were retiring late at night and then go to his room. He actually would want to enter and stay a little in her room but Obaedo feared negative publicity and would tell him 'good night' at the door. But by the second week, when they had settled down, she allowed him into her room. She had found him to be a very interesting person. One thing would lead to another and from that night, she started having an affair with him. She was in that powerful mood to fulfill her body's urges with someone else. Strangely, she felt no remorse. She was somehow cut off from Billy and found Dr. Glenmore a nice company. They would continue on with their conversations and sometimes intimacy. By this time she had judged herself as not being good enough for Billy anymore; that she was no more his standard.

Perhaps it was the turn down for the child dedication, the abject rejection that snapped her or it was the overwhelming loneliness but she just got carried away by this charming young man's company. Until the Bishop gave her a cold silence on dedicating her baby, she had never fully gauged the level of cruelty and wickedness inherent in that church system. Not only were her eyes now opened to see through the whole charade, she saw everything as lost cause.

Back in Benin, she started having another affair with a young handsome member of the state House of Assembly. He would come pick her up from the office after official hours and they would go to town. Sometimes, his car would still be in her compound at 11pm. Although other men later propositioned her for outings, she starting turning them down after breaking up with the state legislator. Like something came over her and she somewhat began to see the emptiness in all this, began to feel real remorseful and called it off. She even attended service once in Deacon Ugo's new church.

She had not told Billy of her dalliances. Billy himself had become so into his law practice though still a very fervent member of his father's church. However, one Sunday she just felt the need to visit the Baptist church of Rev. Onwundinjo with her baby. Billy and her parents received her warmly. Billy told her his father can dedicate her baby if she wanted. She agreed and Billy went to tell his father. He sent for her and had a counseling time with her. He agreed to dedicate her baby who was now almost a year old, the next Sunday.

It turned out to be a big ceremony as Chief Ahamioje made sure his friends and business partners stormed the church in their best dresses. Although he had not fully given his word to be around, the governor surprisingly came in with his entourage and the press.

Billy beautifully sang a special song, Alvin Slaughter's Wonders of His Hands, which he dedicated to Obaedo, drawing huge applause from the congregation.

Morning sun, mountains tall

God above designed them all

Running streams, desert sands

Just a few of the wonders of His hands

I'm amazed when I see

All He's done and to think

He did it all for me

Oh how great, Oh how grand

Are the great and mighty wonders of

His hands

On a hill, on a cross

He stretched out His hands

To save the world so lost

But in the pain was a plan

Yes, this would be the greatest

Wonder of His hands

Broken hearts, torn by sin

With one touch of His hand, new again

Born in love, free to stand

As a glorious new creation of His hands

And I'm amazed when I see

All He's done and to know

He did it all for me

Oh how great to know I am

Standing here as a wonder of His hands

Unashamed I will stand

As a living testimony

To declare the mighty wonders

Wonders of His hands

His mighty hands

They were all touched by the animated Bible sermon of Rev. Onwundinjo which followed this song. He titled his sermon, Redemption, reading from *Romans 3:26, To declare, I say, at this time His righteousness: that He might be just, and the justifier of him which believeth in Jesus.*

And *2 Samuel 14: 14 For we must needs die, and are as water spilt on the ground, which cannot be gathered up again; neither doth God respect any person: yet doth He devise means, that His banished be not expelled from Him.*

"This portion of the Holy Scriptures deals with King David and his son, Absalom, who had murdered his brother and fled into exile. Absalom didn't just kill his brother, Satan had made the young man to defile Absalom's sister and Satan enjoyed the full harvest as the prince was drawn in to commit murder and then lost his home. He was accordingly banished according to the law. What a scheming enemy we have.

This verse of Scripture shows us deeply the Love of God towards those who transgress His Word as the army general Joab devised a way to get Absalom back home. Satan is a great manipulator. He sets traps for men and they fall in. This verse of the Scriptures is the full picture of redemption. God does not respect anybody. Any flesh who breaks His Word reaps the repercussion. Yet when breaking His Word casts us off from Him, this same God devises ways to still draw the estranged sinner back. Oh! How I love Him. What a beauty.

He Himself makes the way for the banished from Him to not be lost forever.

We are gathered here to rejoice with my son's friend of many years, Obaedo Ahamioje.

I have known Obaedo from her early days; I am a friend of her father. Since her secondary school days, she has been a real friend to my son Billy. Young ones here can learn from this, that life is not about all these boyfriend-girlfriend fooling around nonsense. They were disciplined and happy companions. No one can fault the life that this young lady lived. She was a star, she was graceful. Satan conspired to thwart her life's course, to bring reproach upon her testimony and wanted her excommunicated forever from the company of the Saints. She fell into the enemy's trap. Oh! What pain our sister must have been through. She told me that after what happened to her, she sort of hardened up and then dabbled into things she never thought she would ever do. She broke down in my office and wept telling Billy and I things she had done with bitter tears of contrition. She cried that she is no more worthy to be a friend to Billy for the things she had done. She was fully repenting, without any trace of arrogance and feeling worthy in sin. No. There was deep contrition. She wanted her full relationship with God restored. Who am I not to fall down on my knees, rejoice and thank God for such a young woman? My son Billy that brought her to me for her request of what we are doing today can testify. He is a witness that Obaedo gave her heart back to now be serving the God of this Bible, who the Bible tells us is the Justifier of those who believe in Jesus the Word of God. Not believe in subjective impulses and impressions of proud men. No, believe in Jesus Christ. You say you believe in Jesus? Yes, but He is the Christ, the anointed unadulterated Word unhandled by men. Obaedo has given her heart to believe this Jesus the Word of God, to be free from religious servitude to a man's person, to a man's system so self-exalted, that put this precious daughter of God in the mess she was. When men leave God's Word, refuse to humble themselves to God's plain Word and re-interpret it to exalt themselves, they ruin lives of those who follow them and their charming ways. They end up going into superstitious beliefs with no Scriptural foundation and inevitably start indulging in blasphemous fables and dangerous deceit. Obaedo has now experienced Biblical salvation after attending a product of human fiction for years without the bedrock conviction of Biblical Christianity.

If anybody tells you that Obaedo is a wayward girl, don't believe them. Instead pray for that person that he will be saved. Obaedo is a sheep that got caught in the trap of ravenous wolves which the apostle Paul told us would invade the Christian church. She is a lamb who got into a demon-infested neighbourhood and was overpowered in her will and hurt. Then, she snapped, hurt herself more but God Almighty has made a way for her.

The story of this young lady is the story of redemption. And I am so grateful to heaven to have been given the chance to play a role in it.

There are waywards in our churches, hell-bent, so proud, conceited and unwilling to submit to the Word or discipline. They have no interest in having their lives come under this Bible but they just love church atmosphere, they love singing, music and to keep sinning. Church is another social event for them, where they go to pretend and find lovers. That is not Obaedo. Obaedo is a lamb, sheep-natured.

I witness to this congregation that this young woman is banished no more from God's presence. And the God who Himself deviseth ways for the banished to come back to Him, has made the way for Obaedo to come back into His loving arms.

I am going to dedicate her baby named Dawn and pray for our dear sister that God will keep her, make her perfectly whole and bless her tomorrow.

Obaedo, I want to dedicate this portion of Scripture to you, take it for yourself.

Isaiah 44: 21 ¶ Remember these, O Jacob and Israel; for thou art my servant: I have formed thee; thou art my servant: O Israel, thou shalt not be forgotten of me. 22 I have blotted out, as a thick cloud, thy transgressions, and, as a cloud, thy sins: return unto me; for I have redeemed thee.'

Some in the congregation were wiping their eyes with their handkerchief.

After the dedication, the governor was asked to say something to the gathered people.

"I am not much of a church man but what I saw here today gripped me. I fought tears repeatedly. This lady that attracted this huge gathering today, my friend's daughter, is also my daughter. I remember some years back giving her an award as best behaved girl in her secondary school along with Reverend's son as best behaved boy. And the best behaved boy has kept on and was the one instrumental to this event today. Despite what she had been through, the best behaved boy still stood for her. Reverend, you have a gem as a son. Chief Ahamioje, you have a gem for a daughter. I know how Chief Ahamioje is concerned about his children's welfare. But in as much as he did his best, the enemy still slipped in to try to destroy this precious life. I am happy in my heart that there was a preacher of the Gospel, an exemplary minister who was positioned to address this situation, to get himself ready to be used by God to remedy this life. I am told the back ground of this sordid event but see how God used His agent, Rev. Onwundinjo to combact the enemy from having total victory over this young girl, from making her go to pieces. I believe there are places of worship that would have made a hotter hell for her by further complicating her life.

Obaedo, my little advice for you is try to forget what these people have done to you. Find grace to erase it from your heart and move on. It is not easy but leave it to God to handle those who think they can crush others, destroy others and yet under the cloak of religious infallibility, show no remorse, no contrition. Let them continue. Someday, they will meet their Maker. Be like David who refused to smite King Saul his enemy even though he had him by the throat.

I have found that in trying to turn a bad situation around, instead of having total support from all, there are people who will be attacking you to destroy you. Why will a young promising girl go to church to become a better person but instead is almost destroyed in a church? Why? It is the same enemy whose only preoccupation is fighting what will become good, fighting light. Most people blame the devil but he can only work through agents who submit to his devilish interests. It is time ministers of the Gospel rediscover why they are in the ministry. The Gospel was given by Christ to bring light to lives not to make preachers wealthy, megalomaniac and pulpit dictators to destroy others. And leaders of a country must bring light to their people or stay out of power. Like preachers in the pulpit, all who go into power over a people will one day give account. What is your motive in trying to get power? Just to lord over people? One lesson people must take from the experience of this young girl is, whenever you find a church you are in, so-called churches of today, becoming domineering, so full of excessive control of people that you have to take permission to breathe, the red lights should be beeping for you. When what you seeing, not the rhetoric that tingles your ears. No. When what you are seeing as behavior, as conduct, is not natural, does not correspond to the Life that Jesus Christ would live, it is time for you to run! I say run! Run Fast! Don't hang around another moment. You will be consumed. Don't linger there because their rhetoric pretty much gets heated up like their genitals.

I have done my bit in trying to improve this state since I became governor. The forces that could have destroyed me have not succeeded. Those same forces through men in another realm also tried to destroy Obaedo and they failed with both of us."

The congregation burst into applause.

He then invited everyone to the Government House right away for lunch.

"Let the celebrations continue for Obaedo and myself."

The governor then broke out into a local Yoruba praise song and with his huge frame moving back and forth, the congregation joined:

Agbara Esu da ni bi ti Jesu gbe n'joba
Agbara Esu da
Kosi O
O ti wo

{What power does the devil have, where Jesus is Ruling?
Where is the devil's power? There is none...It is destroyed}

Chapter 16
A Plane in the cloud.

During the English week of the English department, the executive of the English Students Association had invited various successful alumni of the department. Among those invited was an alumnus who had made a first-class and was now lecturing at Harvard. He gave an incisive talk to the students and Obaedo was called upon to give the closing remarks. She was inspired by the talk and also by this young dashing lecturer, Dr. Anthony Omatsola.

"The Appointments and Promotions Committee sometimes seem only to be employing lecturers these days just to help cut the unemployment figures down. I can't think of another reason for employing people with the mentality of market men and women to lecture young undergraduates. The lowering of academic standards, the deliberate turning of blind eye to examination cheating by university authorities inevitably destroys lives, it destroys a country. Half-baked doctors will kill thousands; substandard lawyers will corrupt judges and destroy evidence, and when they lobby corrupt politicians and are made Judges, they pervert justice freely; unsound engineering graduates will build substandard projects that will take lives and cause loss of resources; thieving accountants spread their corrupt practices. The university is the gate to a decent and thriving society. What we all saw today from our guest speaker, no doubt inspires all of us that there is a standard we can aspire to. I believe that all of us here were set alight by his beautiful remark, 'Give a man a match, and he'll be warm for a minute, but set him on fire, and he'll be warm for the rest of his life.' That was very apt Dr. Omatsola."

The audience applauded.

She used her words well and he was impressed. After the event, Dr. Omatsola had a chat with her outside, trying to know her better. They just hit it off as their intellect and wit blended. He insisted on taking her out for dinner later that evening. He was supposed to be in the country for a week but he spent an extra week, visiting Obaedo at home and taking her out on dates. She just sensed he was a decent fellow. Some of her friends and department colleagues got wind of it but were never judgmental. They knew this could be something real for a girl who had literally gone through Hell.

Dr. Anthony Omatsola was the second child of a retired university professor of International Relations. His father, an Itsekiri from the Niger Delta, had once served as the Director of the Joint Admissions and Matriculation Board, JAMB. His wife Kemi, is from the wealthy family of Olorunoba in Badagry, Lagos. After his retirement from the University of Benin, he had relocated to Lagos, where he continued as a visiting professor in the University of Lagos and gives Talks around the world.

Obaedo and Dr. Anthony continued communicating on his return back to the United States. Billy had come to see her one day and she was real nice to him although their original spark had yet to return. She confided in him about Dr. Anthony. Billy could only say after a brief pause and a deep sigh,

"Let the Will of God be done."

Just as she had once looked upon the student Woke with pity, she felt deep pity for Billy. She almost cried. But time seemed to have moved on for her. She just lost the feeling and belief that she could be that queen for this amazing young man. She decided that he was now further above her than the moon. She knew Billy was hurt by the path she was now choosing but she had peace within as she saw him handle it just like he always did, a perfect gentleman.

The society wedding of Dr. Anthony and Obaedo took place on December 17th, 2011, in Lagos. He had visited Nigeria again six months after his initial visit to see her father. With her father's permission, he took her out dining one night to a choice restaurant in the city. After the preliminary snack, he knelt down, handing her a ring and saying, "Obaedo, two of us can start all over again, please make me a part of your life. I see in you a road that I should take."

Onlookers clapped while Obaedo covered her face with her hands. She had inklings for this but not the way it came. Overjoyed at her reply, Dr. Anthony ordered meal for everyone in the restaurant. Some young men there, made a song with their names, singing it and striking a rhythm on the table:

Anthony o. Obaedo o

O! O! O! We hail o

The cream of the society was present at the wedding. Governor Edeniyere was there in person along with his wife, his twin daughters who were now married and many members of the state cabinet; the Lagos state governor came too. The federal minister of Housing, the redoubtable chief Femi Maja-Pearse; the Vice chancellor of the University of Benin, Professor Ambrose Oliha; Obaedo's Dean and head of department, colleagues from her department and some of her students were present. Dr. Emily Okpaise was present too and broke down sobbing in joy. Ameze who had been in London for her doctorate programme had kept calling Obaedo throughout the preparation, congratulating and encouraging her.

"Your happiness is important to me baby girl", she would say.

She had also been telling Obaedo about this black British young man with the British Secret Service who had been on her continually.

"By now he should get a medal for all the text messages and pet names he calls me. The last one he called me was 'Strawberry Queen'. Before that was, 'Caribbean Queen,' 'Liberian girl', 'The spy who loved me.'

Obaedo laughed.
"He once told me that am like a brook, a little stream. And when I told that that was the meaning of my name, he went emotional. Is he my soul mate? Don't know but I admire his person. I know best relationships grow up. We'll see. As a woman I am taught to and inclined to distrust men. But this one…"

"It makes me happy to know he has a decent personality and attitude.", Obaedo had told her.

'Yea, he has. Classy and elegant. He is a gentleman and not one with lecherous eyes and going for only one thing. He wants to dine out with me every Saturday as if he will help me in writing my thesis later."

"But that will give you the chance to read him more."

"When did he turn into a book to be read? Anyway I am a good judge of character. He is very enlightened and nice, the epitome of good looks and brain. He said am the only thing in the world that he wants. I then asked him, 'what of pay day?'"

"Ame!"

"Yes na. When men are carried away, they can say most anything. But am watching him, kinda like his kind. Am a little stubborn to him and he seems to like that too."

They both laughed.

"I guess you have charmed him enough for him to be telling
you top government secrets."

"Some. But the bottom line is never believe what you read in the newspapers. Governments everywhere are Machiavellian syndicates."

"I sensed that. But for him to let you in into such hidden fact so early in the relationship means you already have your grip on him."

"No, my claws."

"Ame! I used to figure secret service personnel as stiffs. Is he the type you can sit with in the same room and text each other for fun?" Obaedo asked.

"All through the night."

"He has swept you off your feet then."

"Into the Atlantic really."

Dr. Anthony and his wife spent their honeymoon in Ghana and later in Nigeria. When he had to return back, he was also going to work her papers for her and her baby's relocation to the United States. When the papers were finally ready, she started putting her things together to leave the country. One of those days she decided to invite Billy to her house to tell him the news personally. She made him his favourite meal. Billy wished her the best and insisted on flying down to Lagos to see her off. She reluctantly agreed.

Her flight was by 7pm on a Saturday. She was there by 5pm and completed her boarding formalities. Her father and his wives were also there. They were chatting freely. Joy was in their midst. Just before the time for boarding, Arekha Franklin's (You Make Me Feel Like) A Natural Woman, was playing out on the Public Address System.

Looking out on the morning rain

I used to feel so uninspired

And when I knew I had to face another day

Lord, it made me feel so tired

Before the day I met you, life was so unkind

But you're the key to my peace of mind.

Cause you make me feel, you make me feel, you make me feel like

A natural woman.

Obaedo looked into Billy's eyes. There were a thousand words in that look. She immediately turned away her eyes to the floor. She was weeping.

When my soul was in the lost-and-found

You came along to claim it

I didn't know just what was wrong with me

Till your kiss helped me name it

Now I'm no longer doubtful of what I'm living for

And if I make you happy I don't need to do more

Cause you make me feel, you make me feel, you make me feel like

A natural woman.

Oh, baby, what you've done to me? (What you've done to me?)

You make me feel so good inside (good inside)

And I just wanna be (wanna be)

Close to you, you make me feel so alive

You make me feel

You make me feel

You make me feel like a natural woman (woman)

You make me feel

You make me feel

You make me feel like a natural woman (woman)

When it was announced over the public address that passengers on her flight should proceed to Terminal E62 to start boarding, Obaedo got up and pulled Billy aside. She handed him a little envelope. She gave him a tight hug, the first she ever gave him and whispered in his ears, "I'll never forget you."

Billy was moved. "Thank you for fifteen plus years of unadulterated friendship," he said, looking into her eyes. He shook her hand warmly.

Obaedo hugged her father and his wives one by one, thanking them for their help in her travails. Her mom was wiping her eyes. Then she hugged the dutiful Anita and carried her baby from her. Finally, she waved at Billy.

It wasn't long before they all saw her plane take off. They all waved at it. Billy watched the plane until it disappeared in the clouds taking away something he knew he will forever miss.

He was to take the morning flight back to Benin. Returning back to his hotel room, he took a warm bath, got into bed, pulled the blanket. With only the bed lamp on, he opened her envelope.

March 10th, 2012.

My dear Bill, by the time you read this, I will be air borne on my way to start a new life, a life different from the dear one that you and I have shared together for almost twenty years. You were the first love that I had. You always will be. You gave me the clutches early in life that I held onto to support myself. You were always there to support me throughout my growing up years to becoming a young woman.

Growing up as a young girl, I never knew that I could love someone as much as I came to love you. I heard of love but couldn't figure it out. In you I saw what it really is. I can't really even use the word love because what you showed me is beyond words. You are a complete gentleman Bill.

From those days we shared at Edokpolor Grammar School, staying back to read in the library, walking home together, nothing was going to be the same again in my life, because you had come into my world, into my life. I was never bored when you were around and I had wished that you were my brother to stay in our house.

I wish that you were here now, holding me tight, and that we were travelling together to the States to start our new world that you once wrote to me about. But things have conspired to rob you of being next to me now. Instead I carry my baby, an icon from my former life. I wish you were her dad. Things conspired to rob her of that too; things made me no more good enough for you. I am pained that I let you down but I know you have forgiven me. I am strengthened that you had it in you to forgive me and would move on without me. I never knew life would take me this way. Never thought I would but I went with other guys. I am ashamed to admit it. But I want you to know that my love for you was a pure love. It don't compare.

This is a chance for me to start over. It was painful but I had to let you go. You will find joy Billy. You will find your queen someday. She will fit into you as you fitted into my life. And that will bring me great joy too because you will be happy. I remember the happiness you brought me, your many encouragement through the years and your advice. You helped me solve my problems and made me so much better.

I really liked you Billy. I do. I remember days I couldn't stand not talking to you. You wouldn't believe it but I looked forward to school most times just because of meeting you.

The last three years were a wreck for me. I made a mess of us. But your calmness through it all brought me back my smile until providence decided my fate. So though I start a new life without you, just know this, having met you is one of the best things in my life.

And to quote William Shakespeare, 'And whether we shall meet again I know not. Therefore our everlasting farewell take. Forever and forever farewell. If we do meet again, why, we shall smile. If not, why then this parting was well made.'

Billy, we will always have Upper Lawani. I say thank you for loving me. Thank you for caring. Thank you for your kindness. Thank you for being yourself at all times. Thank you for always making me happy. Thank you for always finding a way to make me feel better. Thank you for sharing your time. Thank you for those words of strength. Thank you for being so helpful. Thank you for everything! I never once faced you and said it, but I love you till tomorrow, Barrister William Chukwuemeka Onwundinjo.

Your Oba.

Cliff Chima

www.ingramcontent.com/pod-product-compliance
Lightning Source LLC
Chambersburg PA
CBHW021101080526
44587CB00010B/331